INSIGHTS
ON LEARNING DISABILITIES

An International Journal
published by Learning Disabilities Worldwide

Mission Statement

Insights on Learning Disabilities *mission is to provide the most-up-to-date information on intervention, diagnosis, and management in the field of Learning Disabilities in such a way that is accessible to those interested in translating prevailing theories into effective daily practices. Insights articles aim to support individuals with learning disabilities, their families, and the professionals in the field.*

INSIGHTS
ON LEARNING DISABILITIES

An International Journal
published by Learning Disabilities Worldwide

TABLE OF CONTENTS

PUBLISHER
Learning Disabilities Worldwide (LDW) LDW Website: http://www.ldworldwide.org
SUBSCRIPTION RATES—bi-annual publication—US currency only—includes shipping and handling
Individual/Family—$40
Professional—$60
Institutional—$100
International—Canada, Europe, and South America—$75
International—all others—$120
ELECTRONIC VERSION (IN PDF) IS AVAILABLE for $30.00

EDITORIAL POLICY

Learning Disabilities Worldwide publishes the journal, *Insights on Learning Disabilities* (ILD), twice yearly. The purpose of this publication is to provide the most up-to-date information on the practices of assessment, educational support, and psychosocial intervention that are available for individuals with learning disabilities. *Insights on Learning Disabilities* recognizes as a main part of its mission the requirement to report on the educational services and the social opportunities that may be of benefit to individuals with learning disabilities. Consistent with this recognition, *Insights on Learning Disabilities* publishes high-quality articles describing assessment techniques, instructional practices, program developments, and teaching materials addressing the needs of individuals with learning disabilities. Other materials that ILD also considers appropriate for publication are opinion papers on policy and legislation matters pertaining LD. Of special interest are works that help researchers, practitioners, and parents understand how the prevailing theories on the different aspects of learning disabilities can be translated into daily practice in the environments where individuals with LD are evaluated and supported. The following guidelines will help authors to prepare their manuscripts for consideration of publication in *Insights on Learning Disabilities.*

The types of articles considered appropriate for publication in ILD are:

Empirical studies with an applied focus. Papers presenting research findings with a strong emphasis on implications for practice are considered appropriate for ILD.
Authors of these papers should adhere to the writing guidelines described in the 5th Edition of the Publication Manual of the American Psychological Association (APA). The length of the manuscript should be between 12–25 typewritten, double-spaced pages, including tables, figures, references, and appendices.

Small sample size and case studies. Reports on the effectiveness of innovative techniques and procedures implemented with small samples but based on sound theoretical grounds and using valid designs, could be regarded as appropriate for publication. The length of the manuscript should be between 12–25 typewritten, double-spaced pages, including tables, figures, references, and appendices.

Papers with guidelines for parents. Papers presenting research-based guidelines for successfully parenting children with LD will be considered, provided that they include systematic explanations and propose carefully documented and unambiguous responses to parental concerns. The length of the manuscript should be between 10–20 typewritten, double-spaced pages, including figures, references, and appendices.

Investigations on personnel preparation. Investigations on effective models of initial and in-service training of personnel working with students with LD will be considered for publication, provided that they include details on the specific practices as well as the theoretical background of the program. The length of the manuscript should be between 10–20 typewritten, double-spaced pages, including tables, figures, references, and appendices.

Critical Reviews of literature on LD. Reviews of literature dealing with subjects pertinent to LD may be accepted in the journal, if they are well documented in terms of theory and methodology. The length of the manuscript should be between 12–25 typewritten, double-spaced pages.

PUBLISHER Continued

Papers addressing topics pertinent to adults with LD. Papers addressing areas such as professional, vocational, academic or social opportunities for adults with LD or any other aspect of the responsibilities of community membership, may be accepted in the journal, if they include systematic explanations research-based or unambiguous guidelines. The length of the manuscript should be between 10–20 typewritten, double–spaced pages, including figures, references, and appendices.

Hardware/software reviews. Recently released technological innovations pertinent to LD can be reviewed and considered for publication. The length and the technical details of such publications should be discussed with the editors for guidance prior to submission.

Theme issues. ILD welcomes theme issues. Individuals are encouraged to propose themes to the editors and either identify participant authors or consult with the editors to place an open call for submissions.

MANUSCRIPT SUBMISSION.

Electronic submissions are encouraged at either iagal@uom.gr or tacitro@aol.com .
Submissions via regular mail (4 copies) may be sent to either Ioannis Agaliotis, Ph.D., or to Teresa Allissa Citro at Learning Disabilities Worldwide, P.O. Box 142,Weston, MA 02493. Authors must send a cover letter with their submissions indicating the title and length of the paper and must state that their work is not currently under review in another journal. The first page of the manuscript should include the title of the article and the complete names and institutional affiliations of the authors, as well as a short title to be used as a running head, whereas a second page should indicate only the title. Each article should be prefaced by a brief abstract (120–160 words). Authors should also include a short (40–60 words) biographical statement with the heading.

Manuscripts will be sent for a blind review to two to three members of the editorial board and authors will be informed on the editorial decision with a formal letter from one of the editors. If the manuscript is accepted, the authors will be asked to send it electronically as a Word 2000 (both PC and Mac formats are acceptable) and they also must complete a copyright waiver form. The editors reserve the right to make final editorial changes to the manuscript without however altering the content of the original submission.

Articles are judged on the following criteria: importance of the article to the field, soundness of conceptualization, adequacy of the research, reliability of conclusions and style of writing. In reference to the last criterion, authors are encouraged to use an appealing style, avoiding jargon and "academic prose", so that the manuscript provides all readers with as many *Insights on Learning Disabilities* as possible.

CORRECTION

In the paper, *Neurofeedback Treatment of Two Children with Learaning Disabilities and Attention Deficit Hyperactivity Disorder,* by Edward H. Jacobs, vol 2(1), 18–30, 2005, the last sentence that begins on page 27 and continues on page 28 should read: "At the end of the treatment, all of the problems were rated as occurring 'Just a little.'"

Insights on Learning Disabilities 2(2), 1-10, 2005

Reading Development and Suggestions for Teaching Reading to Students with Learning Disabilities

Patricia Gildroy
Portland State University

Donald D. Deshler
University of Kansas

What is reading, and why is it so difficult to learn to read for many individuals with learning disabilities? These questions have plagued the field of education for decades. After years of focused research, researchers are finding answers. This two article series gives a broad overview of the development of reading, the challenges individuals with reading disabilities face, and the types of interventions needed to help struggling readers become stronger readers. This article addresses the ramifications of poor reading skills, the major components in learning to read, characteristics of students with learning disabilities, and the stages of word recognition. The second article Volume 3, No. 1 primarily focuses on reading comprehension.

Ramifications of Poor Reading

The ramifications of struggling to read can be devastating. Even first and second grade struggling readers notice they can't do what most of their peers can do; read words, read stories, read books. Teachers and families become concerned. Other children notice. Some peers ridicule. The struggling readers wonder why they can't read. Is there something terribly wrong with them? Maybe it is their fault. Should they be working harder or doing something differently? Or, are they "defective"?

Struggling to learn to read *is not the fault* of the children, yet it can make going to school very painful. Nearly 80% of children identified with learning disabilities have reading disabilities. As they move through the grades, if these children do not receive intensive, systematic, and explicit instruction in reading, they may give up. They grow tired of not being able to read and make sense of textbooks. They grow tired of "failing." A conservative estimate is that approximately 10% of students with learning disabilities drop out of high school each year in the U.S.

While many individuals with learning disabilities compensate for reading difficulties and become successful in their chosen vocations, many more face great challenges as adults. Employment wages for jobs that don't require reading are predominantly low and may not support growing families. With few or no benefits and less preventative health care, greater health issues surface for the poor readers who may hold these types of positions than for their better reading peers. Tragically, of the people incarcerated in the U.S., approximately 80% are poor readers. This trajectory is unacceptable. Educators and families can work as partners to help individuals with reading disabilities become better readers. To begin, these partners need a basic understanding of what reading is and what the processes and skills involved in learning to read are. They also require an understanding of how to provide the kind of instruction struggling readers need to become strong readers.

What is reading and why do some people struggle with learning to read?

One way to define reading is: the ability to translate an abstract written code into words and sentences while simultaneously and flexibly using comprehension strategies to understand the writer's meaning. Gough and Tunmer (1986) illustrated this relationship with their Simple View of Reading (Figure 1). Using a math analogy, if a score of 10 equals an average score, and a score of 2 is a very low score, the factor of word-recognition proficiency (WRP) *times* the factor of language-comprehension proficiency (LCP) equals the *product,* reading-comprehension proficiency (RCP). The mathematrical representation of this concept is (WRP x LCP = RCP). A weakness in either factor yields a smaller product.

Language comprehension × Word Recognition = Reading Comprehension

Figure 1. The simple view of reading

Individuals with word recognition difficulties will have trouble with reading comprehension even if they are very smart, have extensive vocabularies, and converse at high levels; this is true dyslexia (see Table 1). Likewise, those who are very strong in word recognition but have poor language comprehension will have poor reading comprehension; this is hyperlexia. There are also individuals with poor word recognition and poor language comprehension, which result in poor reading comprehension. Some speech/language pathologists may consider these individuals to be language learning disabled. Understanding this helps, but questions remain. Why do these students have difficulty learning to read?

Biomedical research is beginning to shed some light on the answers. Using functional magnetic resonance imaging (MRI), Shaywitz (2003) conducted a series of studies comparing the brain activity during reading of individuals with and without reading disabilities. She found strong differences between these groups of individuals in both the intensity and the location of their brain activity during reading. To date it is unclear if these differences occur because of reading difficulties, or if they may contribute to reading difficulties. Shaywitz also conducted functional MRIs with individuals with reading disabilities before and after receiving research-based reading instruction that was explicit, responsive, systematic, and intensive. Not only did these individuals become better readers, their brain activity became more intensive in the same areas as the stronger readers. Shaywitz and many other reading researchers are getting exciting results in their studies that are identifying the critical characteristics of the type of intensive, explicit instruction that truly can help most individuals with reading disabilities become stronger readers. The more that educators are able to familiarize themselves with the research, the more they will be able to improve their instruction. Having a thorough understanding of the knowledge and skills required for proficient reading is essential.

Table 1
Broad Reading Disability Subtypes Using Language Comprehension and Word Recognition

Word Recognition	X	Language Comprehension	=	Reading Comprehension	Reading Disability Subtype
Good (10)	X	Good (10)	=	Good (100)	Good
Poor (2)	X	Good (10)	=	Poor (20)	Dyslexic
Good (10)	X	Poor (2)	=	Poor (20)	Hyperlexic
Poor (2)	X	Poor (2)	=	Very Poor (4)	Language-Learning Disability

Overview of Reading Comprehension Components

Building on Gough and Tunmer's Simple View of Reading (1986), the conceptual map of reading (Figure 2) highlights major components of word recognition and language and text comprehension that comprise reading comprehension. This map is an adaptation of the map developed by the Online Academy Jurors, who were advisers on the development of online modules on Teaching Reading to Individuals with Reading Disabilities. Jurors Joe Torgeson, Joe Jenkins, Michael Pressley, Hugh Catts, Joanna Williams, Candace Bos, Anita Archer, and Arlene Barry were selected as advisors because of their areas of expertise as researchers and educators in the field of reading disabilities. Through a series of dynamic discussions, these jurors developed a conceptual map of reading and identified the critical research for each area. This map became the source of the information in the online modules and in this article.

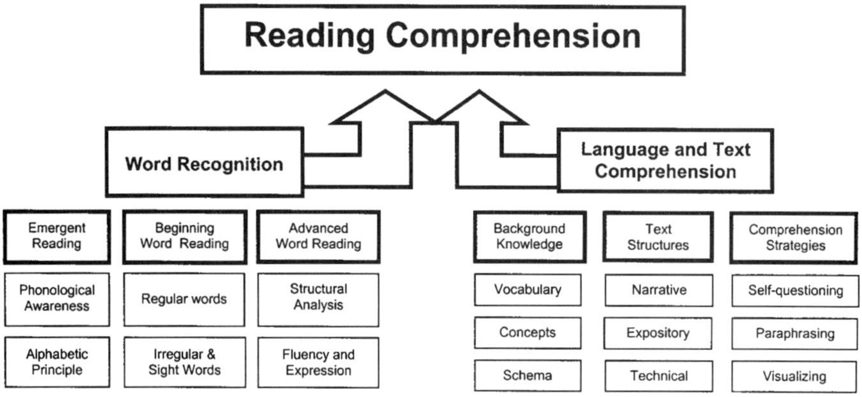

Figure 2. Major components of reading comprehension

Both of the components of reading comprehension, Word Recognition and Language and Text Comprehension, are described briefly here. Part one of this two-article series discusses Word Recognition in more detail. Part two of the series examines Language and Text Comprehension more fully.

The Word Recognition portion of the map illustrates children in the Emergent Reading Stage as learning how to use language to convey meaning. Two of the many critical foundation skills children need to learn are (a) phonological awareness, which is understanding spoken words can be broken or segmented into smaller speech sounds that can be manipulated to change the meaning of words; and (b) the alphabetic principle, which is understanding that individual letters represent speech sounds and combinations of letters can represent spoken words. These tend to be difficult concepts for individuals with reading disabilities. Beginning readers then learn how to interpret different combinations of letters starting with words in which letters make their most common sounds. Soon, they learn to read irregular and sight words they will see in the stories they read and in other materials. As students move through the grades, the vocabulary becomes more difficult. Students must use structural analysis to learn to segment long words into parts so they can read new words more accurately. Throughout each stage of word recognition, students benefit from fluency development to cement the foundation skills upon which their reading comprehension is dependent. Students with reading disabilities need explicit, systematic, research-based, responsive instruction with many opportunities for the students to have successful practice while mastering these skills.

On the Language and Text Comprehension side of the map, rich language environments and experiences help young children to build their background knowledge including vocabulary, concepts, and schemas about how the world works. Readers also need to know about different text structures. Narratives, stories and novels, have specific structures that differ from those in expository or informational texts. The narrative text structure of a story helps readers to anticipate the series of problems that lead to the major problem, climax, and resolution. With expository structure knowledge, readers use the general organization of content texts (e.g., science and health) to preview before reading, to review what they read, and to find information they want. Strong readers also use many comprehension strategies including self-questioning to check their understanding, predict what will come next, and compare that with their prior knowledge. Paraphrasing is required for taking notes and for processing and remembering what is read, as well as for many other life activities. Visualizing, or making pictures in one's mind, helps bring the author's writing to life. What does it look like, how does it sound? What did the author see in his or her mind's eye when writing? Visualizing also helps in many other life activities such as walking or driving routes, building, sewing, cooking, and the creative arts.

Reading is not an isolated task. Strong readers simultaneously, fluently, and silently use their knowledge of the world and their reading skills to comprehend what they read. How did they learn to do this? Estimates say that 20% of students have the capacity to learn to read regardless of the type of instruction they receive. Another 60% of students need to learn the foundations of reading including phonics to become strong readers. With the emphasis on using research-based instructional methods, elementary teachers are being better prepared to provide this type of instruction. Yet, estimations are that the remaining 20% of students need more than what is provided in typical classrooms. An even smaller proportion of students, those with reading disabilities, require intensive, explicit, systematic, and responsive instruction, with attention to all of the above components, in order to build the foundation enabling them to become strong, life-long readers.

Word Recognition

Emergent Literacy

The emergent phase of reading begins right after babies are born. Infants are primed to learn the language of their parents. Regardless of the country in which an infant is born, all infants use the same speech sounds when they first babble. After immersion in their family's language, infants' babble begins to incorporate the speech sounds and intonations they hear in their homes. This is one of the first signs of language learning.

As toddlers accumulate experiences with their primary language, they begin to produce somewhat intelligible speech using nouns and short phrases. At this stage, toddlers may recognize individual words as discrete units of speech that carry meaning. Most children take several years to consistently produce messages that include the proper syntax (word order and word forms such as ran vs. runned) to convey the intended meaning. During this time, children quickly learn and begin to incorporate new vocabulary words as their language usage becomes more sophisticated. These children might also begin to notice that written symbols carry meaning.

Children in literate families have many opportunities to listen to strong language models. They see adults and older children read to gain information and enjoyment. They see readers looking at strange symbols in newspapers, books, signs, food products, and television commercials. The symbols even appear in the written form of the children's names. Soon after, most children learn what large symbols mean, such as the stop sign, the McDonald© sign, or the word *pizza* on a box. Children may say, "stop" when they see the sign, but may not be able to read the word in a different font and context. Individual letters and written words are not meaningful; they are considered part of the object on which they are affixed. These large symbols become associated with stopping, or eating desired food. Soon, children begin to name specific letters and may even say their sounds, but that doesn't mean they are ready to transfer that knowledge to reading words.

In languages using the Roman alphabet, developing phonological awareness is an important step in the process of becoming a proficient reader. Phonological awareness is being able to segment and manipulate spoken words into smaller parts. For example, *baseball* contains two words, *base* and *ball.* In addition, taking away parts, adding parts, or rearranging word parts can change the meaning. The word *hug* can change to *hugs, hugging,* or *hugged.*

More specifically, phonemes, the smallest speech sounds used in words, can change the meaning of words when manipulated. For instance, *man* is made of three phonemes or sounds /m/a/n/, substituting a /k/ for the /m/ changes the word *man* to the word *can.* Linguists have identified between 39 and 43 phonemes that when combined make up all two million plus words in the English language. Children with strong phonological awareness show much greater skill in reading through the first years of school than do children with poor phonological awareness (Torgesen, Wagner, & Rashotte, 1994; see Share & Stanovich, 1995 for a review). Rhyming games can strengthen these skills. Having children hold up one finger for each sound they hear or move pennies for each sound in a word also helps to develop this understanding.

Preschoolers may learn to sing the alphabet song and may be able to say the names or sounds of letters when they see them. Although these are valuable skills, they are not sufficient for successful beginning reading. Children must understand the complex concepts that: (a) spoken words can be broken apart into individuals sounds, (b) letters represent these sounds, (c) combinations of letters represent words, and (d) by looking at the letters and saying their associated sounds, you can figure out what the written word is. This is the alphabetic principle. Many individuals with reading disabilities lack the skill of being able to break spoken words into their phonemes. Regardless of their age, with much work and practice in identifying phonemes in spoken words, and making the associations between the sounds and the letters that represent them, most of these individuals make great strides in word recognition.

Beginning Word Recognition

When teaching beginning readers who may be at risk for, or who have reading disabilities, instruction needs to be explicit, systematic, and of sufficient duration, for the instructional period. It also must be repeated over time to insure mastery. Beginning readers need to master the letter names and their most commonly used sounds. With explicit instruction, students watch as the teacher points to the letter "s," listen to the teacher say the /s/, and when looking at the "s," say its sound. After practicing a few times, the teacher presents a few previously mastered letters as a discrimination and mastery activity in which students see and say other letter sounds as well as the new sound. Students also practice writing letters when dictated as a beginning spelling activity.

Once students learn a few letters (e.g., s, a, m, r, t) they need to learn to blend, or sound out, consonant-vowel-consonant words (CVC words). Some students with reading disabilities stop between the sounds; they need to say sounds in a continuous flow of breath *(mmmmmmaaaaaannnnnn mmmm-maaaannn man)*. As a reciprocal skill, students can practice spelling by segmenting dictated words and writing the letters. Some students may have trouble recognizing sounds in words such as the "n" in *hand*. Learning to pay attention to what their mouths do when they produce the sounds helps them identify more of the sounds when spelling and may help in reading. With explicit instruction in reading beginning sight words (those without the most common letter sounds such as *he, the, was, is*), students are ready to begin reading connected text. This is a milestone.

Soon beginning readers are ready to learn letter combinations such as digraphs (two letters one sound as in *ai, sh, ch*) and consonant blends (two or more letters two or more sounds as in *cl, nd, str*). Teaching magic "e" words (e.g., *hope, cake*) requires teaching a rule and using discrimination words for practice (e.g., *hope hop, cute cut*). They learn about letters that make more than one sound (e.g., c, g, ea). Learning and practicing spelling rules for adding common suffixes also helps students with word recognition. Throughout this stage, students need to read and write words in isolation, as well as read and write connected text to increase accuracy and fluency. Appropriate texts for students to read at this stage contain the types of words they have learned to read. Material should be at the student's independent reading level (97% accuracy).

If a student is asked to read at his or her instructional level (92% accuracy), there should be a teacher or parent to help with words that are more difficult and to listen as sentences with errors are re-read. Readers should not be expected to independently read materials at their frustrational level (less than 90% accuracy). Not only will this weaken their comprehension, but it also can produce negative feelings about reading. Instead, these readers can follow along as they listen to the material read by others or an audiotape recording. Once readers have mastered basic reading (approximately the 2.5 grade level of reading), they are ready for the next stage.

Advanced Word Reading

Learning to read and write in English is challenging. Although there are only 39 to43 phonemes, there are more than 251 ways to spell those sounds in the millions of words in the English language. Although only 200,000 words are used commonly in English (versus German with 170,000 and French with 100,000), a high percentage of words are derivations (Bryson, 1990). In order to convey meaning, derivational words retain the original root word spelling when adding suffixes and prefixes, although sometimes the pronunciation may change. In addition, words taken directly from other languages frequently retain the original pronunciation rather than change into a more typical phonetic pronunciation in English. To add to the complexity of English, the sounds that letters make change over time and certainly across geographic regions. All of these influences on English make it a very rich language, but a more difficult one to learn to read.

A common myth about individuals with reading disabilities is that their reading skills plateau at the fourth-grade level and cannot increase. Not surprisingly, a large proportion of these students use ineffective strategies for reading longer words. Most teachers would say the typical strategy struggling readers use for decoding multisyllabic words is the "Guess and Go" strategy. Not being able to read long words can be devastating and lead to the school failure and the type of frustration that causes many students to eventually drop out of school. Each year, beginning in the fourth and fifth-grades, textbooks introduce approximately 10,000 words that are new to most students (Nagy & Anderson, 1984). Most of the critical words in textbooks are longer words; students must be able to read and understand these words, or have appropriate accommodations, to learn the content and be successful in school.

When proficient readers come across an unknown word in text, they go through a series of steps to read it. First, they look at each letter in the word and analyze the structure by breaking the word into decodable parts. Next, they say the parts fast and make it into a known word if it is in their oral vocabulary.

Finally, they verify it is the correct word by checking it in the context of the sentence. If the new word is not in their oral vocabulary, they may use the context to determine the meaning or look it up so they will recognize this word the next time they see it. Again, students with reading disabilities need explicit, intensive, responsive, and systematic instruction to master this set of skills. Struggling readers who have learned this multisyllabic word reading strategy often increase their word recognition skills rapidly and significantly, some as much as three or more grade levels (Archer, Gleason, & Vachon, 2000, 2003).

Developing Accuracy and Fluency in Reading

Across each of these phases in word recognition, reading fluency is important. If too much mental energy is devoted to decoding, comprehension suffers, but accuracy should always precede fluency work. Having students practice errors only reinforces the errors, making it more difficult for students to read the words correctly. Recently, numerous materials became available to help readers at all levels increase reading fluency. Having students read the same passage, or listen to others and then practice reading the passage, both show strong results in improving reading fluency.

Early childhood through the first years of school is a critical time for children to learn the foundation skills needed for reading. Students with reading disabilities may have difficulty learning one or all of the components discussed above. Regardless of the age of the struggling readers, finding the areas of difficulty and working to strengthen them will enable the development of these foundation skills. With the addition of vocabulary development, learning about text structures, and using powerful reading comprehension strategies, these individuals are on their way to becoming strong readers. Great effort is required of the students and the teachers; the rewards however, are great. Students with reading disabilities can become successful in school. That success may be the most powerful motivator for students to continue to work toward their high school diploma. In increasingly greater numbers, students with reading disabilities are earning their bachelor's degrees and beyond. Learning to be a strong reader opens doors to the world.

References

Archer, A. L., Gleason, M. M., & Vachon, V. (2000). *Reading excellence: Word attack and rate development strategies (REWARDS).* Longmont, CO: Sopris West.

Archer, A. L., Gleason, M. M., & Vachon, V. L. (2003). Decoding and fluency foundation skills for struggling older readers. *Learning Disability Quarterly, 26*(2), 89–102.

Bryson, B. (1990). *The mother tongue: English and how it got that way.* New York: William Morrow.

Gough, P. B., & Tunmer, W. E. (1986). Decoding, reading, and reading disability. *Remedial and Special Education, 7*(1), 6–10.

Nagy, W. E., & Anderson, R. C. (1984). How many words are there in printed school English? *Reading Research Quarterly, 19*(3), 304–330.

Share, D. L. & Stanovich, K. E. (1995). Cognitive processes in early reading development: A model of acquisition and individual differences. *Issues in Education: Contributions from Educational Psychology, 1,* 1–57.

Shaywitz, S. (2003). *Overcoming dyslexia: A new and complete science-based program for reading problems at any level.* New York: Alfred A. Knopf.

Torgesen, J. K., Wagner, R. K., & Rashotte, C. A. (1994). Longitudinal studies of phonological processing and reading. *Journal of Learning Disabilities, 27,* 276–286.

Insights on Learning Disabilities 2(2), 11–22, 2005

My Child Can't Read: What Should I Do?

Howard Margolis, Ed.D.
Queens College of CUNY

If your child struggles with reading, you have good reason to worry. After all, struggling readers usually feel humiliated and ashamed about their "failure." They're often badgered to try harder, although they start out working hard, trying their best. Some, desperately wanting to read, struggle endlessly, in vain, while others resist reading and eventually drop out of school. As adults, few compete successfully in a world requiring ever increasing literacy abilities. Fortunately, with proper support and instruction, many struggling readers can become good readers. And legally, schools must help.

Although many schools want to help, many don't. If they don't, three federal laws give you leverage if your child meets their "technical" eligibility definitions. Roughly speaking, if your child's reading difficulties are moderate-to-severe, he may be eligible for special education under the Individuals with Disabilities Education Act of 2004 (IDEA); if they're mild-to-moderate, Section 504 of the Rehabilitation Act of 1973 (Section 504) and the No Child Left Behind Act of 2001 (NCLB) can often help.[1]

The Three Laws

Eligible for Special Education under the Individuals with Disabilities Education Act of 2004 (IDEA)

A full eligibility evaluation. Under IDEA, schools must evaluate children suspected of having reading disabilities, to determine their eligibility for special education and their educational needs. Thus, you have the right to request an evaluation to determine your child's eligibility and needs. Fortunately, the process can be relatively quick. IDEA requires that your school district complete the evaluation within 60 days of your consent (unless your state has a different time frame), and that a team of "qualified professionals" evaluate your child, using a variety of technically sound measures or assessments.

IDEA also gives you the right to request a comprehensive evaluation by a reading specialist. Because schools rarely provide a reading specialist's evaluation, request one. If schools will not provide a comprehensive reading evaluation, show them these sections of IDEA: "Each local education agency (LEA) shall ensure

---

[1] For more precise definitions of eligibility, parents are urged to read the federal laws and regulations. These, along with informative articles on the laws, can be found at www.nichcy.org (the National Dissemination Center for Children with Disabilities). For IDEA, parents are also urged to read their state laws and regulations.

that . . . Assessments . . . are administered by trained and knowledgeable personnel . . . The child is assessed in all areas of suspected disability . . . Assessment tools and strategies . . . provide relevant information that directly assists persons in determining the educational needs of the child" (20 U.S.C. §1414, Evaluations and IEPs). Then, if you live in one of the many states that have separate certifications for reading teacher or specialist, remind them that the state recognizes reading as a specific discipline requiring a specific course of study.

The Individualized Education Program (IEP). Shortly after the evaluations are completed, you and the team must meet to determine if your child has a disability that makes him eligible for special education. If your child is ineligible, the school can still use IDEA funds to provide the additional reading help he needs to succeed in general education. Moreover, as discussed below, he may also qualify for extra help under Section 504 and NCLB.

If, however, your child is eligible, his IEP Team must then meet to jointly write a plan, called an Individualized Education Program (IEP), that is likely to meet his special education needs, including teaching him to read.[2] The Team consists of a school representative,[3] at least one special education teacher, at least one regular education teacher (if your child does or may participate in general education settings, such as a general education class), a professional qualified to interpret the implications of the evaluation results, people with knowledge or special expertise about your child, your child (if appropriate), and you.[4] Because the reading specialist is probably the only person "who can interpret the instructional implications of the [reading] evaluation" (IDEA, 20 U.S.C. §1414, Evaluations and IEPs), you should formally request the specialist's attendance.

IDEA's meaningful progress benefit. As part of the IEP, the school must provide whatever services (other than services that are clearly medical, that require a doctor or hospital) your child needs to make significant progress in reading. Of course, to obtain these services, justification is needed.

The word "meaningful" is important—federal courts have not allowed schools to offer programs likely to produce only trivial or insignificant progress. The services in the IEP must offer your child the likelihood of making progress consistent with his abilities, progress likely to achieve the goals in his IEP. This is one reason why IDEA now requires that special education programs be

---

[2] This article does not fully discuss IEPs. For more comprehensive information about IEPs, visit www.nichcy.org or www.ed.gov

[3] IDEA requires that the representative be (a) knowledgeable about the availability or resources and the general education curriculum, and (b) qualified to provide or supervise special education. Insist that the representative attend, as only he or she may have the authority to commit resources.

[4] You, as parent or guardian, are an equal member of the team. Your thoughts, suggestions, and concerns are as important as anyone else's. Moreover, IDEA mandates that the IEP Team consider the parents' concerns for enhancing their child's education.

"based on peer reviewed research to the extent practicable" (IDEA, 20 U.S.C. §1414, Evaluations and IEPs). This is also why he needs a reading evaluation that accurately and comprehensively portrays his needs and abilities, and why the goals in his IEP must be ambitious, but realistic. "Ambitious, but realistic" is an educational phrase, coined by the author; it means that with (a) quality instruction, using programs and instructional strategies that reflect the findings of peer-reviewed research, and (b) with continued, reasonable effort by your child, he will likely make substantial progress in reading, progress sufficient to achieve his IEP goals.

The core. The IEP is the core of every child's special education program. By law, it is a highly personalized, mandated document that must describe your child's "present levels of academic achievement and functional performance," list "measurable annual goals, including academic and functional goals, designed to . . . enable [your] child to be involved in and make progress in the general education curriculum [including reading]," list whatever related services and supplementary aids and services your child needs to obtain these goals, list the supports your child's teachers and other school personnel need to help him achieve these goals, and specify the school and type of setting(s) in which your child will be placed. (20 U.S.C. §1414, Evaluations and IEPs). Typical program settings you might be offered include:

- A general education class with an aide or an in-class support teacher to help with reading.
- A general education class with your child pulled-out for reading instruction by a resource or remedial reading teacher.
- A self-contained, full-time special education class.

Whatever the setting, it's critical that the personnel be highly knowledgeable and skilled in the teaching of reading to struggling readers and that they know how to make instruction enjoyable, motivating, and productive. Having a good IEP without knowledgeable, skilled instructional staff is like having a good blueprint for a house, but one built by carpenters, plumbers, and electricians who can't read blueprints. The result: Disaster.

Although IDEA encourages schools to employ "highly qualified" teachers, it does not explicitly mandate that they be effective; moreover, the definition of "highly qualified" is contentious and ambiguous and differs among states. Thus, it's important that you advocate for knowledgeable, skilled instructional staff. One way to do this is to have the IEP Team write an IEP that calls for "— hours weekly of instruction by a certified reading specialist." Another way is to have the IEP state that in order to improve your child's reading, a reading specialist will review his progress weekly, help plan each week's reading instruction, and consult with his teacher—hours weekly. When making one or both of these requests, keep in mind two points: (a) many special education teachers have little formal education in teaching struggling readers how to read; (b) many state's recognize that diagnosing reading difficulties and teaching reading to struggling readers is different from special education; consequently, they offer different certifications.

"*Least Restrictive Environment (LRE).*" IDEA recognizes that no one setting is correct for every child. Thus, IDEA requires that each child's program take place in the Least Restrictive Environment (LRE), one that differs for different children. Specifically, IDEA requires that "to the maximum extent appropriate, children with disabilities . . . are [to be] educated with children who are not disabled, and special classes, separate schooling, or other removal of children with disabilities from the regular educational environment occurs only when the nature or severity of the disability of a child is such that education in regular classes with the use of supplementary aids and services cannot be achieved satisfactorily" (PL 108-446, § 612. State Eligibility). This means that (a) once IEP goals are agreed to, first consideration must be given to placement in general education, with whatever supplementary aids and services your child needs to succeed; (b) your child's program must be sufficiently personalized for him to achieve each of the goals in his IEP; and (c) your child must be educated in settings or classes that are as "normal" as possible, and in which he can achieve his IEP goals.

Legally, schools cannot place your child in a more restrictive environment because a less restrictive one that can fully meet his needs is unavailable or is more expensive. If your child can achieve his IEP goals in a regular class with the daily in-class help of a reading specialist, a special education class would be too restrictive and therefore illegal; in contrast, if your child requires the intensity and non-competitiveness of a specialized school for children with dyslexia to achieve his IEP goals, placement in a regular class with extra help from a reading specialist would be too restrictive, as he is unlikely to make adequate progress. Decisions about the appropriate setting or LRE must always be made on the basis of your child's unique needs, the degree to which the program involves him with children without disabilities, and his ability to make progress in the placement.

A plan that works. In essence, the IEP is a plan agreed to by you and the school's IEP Team members. As such, it must address your child's specific needs, unique abilities, and offer a program likely to produce good gains in reading; by law, it cannot be a generic boilerplate document the school gives to all children with reading disabilities. If the IEP is not working—if your child is not making sufficient progress—you should, in writing, request another IEP meeting, to identify the blocks to learning and to develop a new IEP, one that removes the blocks and provides the services needed to successfully teach your child to read.

But how do you know if the IEP is working, if your child is achieving his goals? IDEA requires that the IEP contain "a description of *how* the child's progress toward meeting the [IEP's] annual goals . . . will be measured and *when* periodic reports on the progress the child is making toward meeting the annual goals . . . will be provided" (20 U.S.C. §1414, Evaluations and IEPs, italics added). A problem with this is that for all but children with the most limiting disabilities, IDEA no longer requires short-term objectives or benchmarks. As part of the IEP Team, however, you can request that (a) the IEP include short-term objectives or benchmarks to answer the how and when requirements; (b) your child's teachers send you the results of weekly Curriculum-Based Measurement (CBM) probes, such as counting the number of words your child correctly pronounces in one minute of passage reading; (c) your child's teachers send you the results of weekly Goal Attainment Scaling, a system they can use to numerically rate his progress in meeting his annual reading goals. If these don't work, consider hiring a reading specialist to assess progress.

Ineligible for Special Education under IDEA

Section 504 of the Rehabilitation Act of 1973 (Section 504). If your child is judged ineligible for special education under IDEA, all is not lost. Specially designated school representatives (usually the original IDEA "team of qualified professionals") must formally meet to determine your child's eligibility for additional or specialized reading services under Section 504 (29 U.S.C. § 794); often, 504's definition of disabilities makes struggling readers eligible. If your child struggles to learn to read, and if progress is poor, she probably meets 504's eligibility definition.[5]

In a nutshell, 504 requires the school to provide your child with the same opportunity to succeed in reading that it provides other children; often, this means additional services. In many respects, however, the services, rights, and potential benefits of IDEA eligibility are greater and more exact than 504 eligibility.[6] One of the major benefits of IDEA, distinguishing it from 504, is that IDEA requires a written IEP that contains specific items, such as annual academic and functional goals and statements of how progress toward these will be measured, and when you will be notified of progress.

The No Child Left Behind Act of 2001 (NCLB). Under the NCLB (115 Stat. 1425, Pub. L. 107-110), schools must demonstrate that each subgroup of students identified by NCLB (e.g., students with disabilities, economically

---

[5] In broad terms, the definition states that schools cannot discriminate against children who have mental or physical problems that "substantially impair or restrict one or more major life activities, such as . . . learning" (Section 504).

[6] This is because IDEA is a "benefits" act and Sections 504 is a civil rights discrimination act.

disadvantaged students) has made adequate yearly progress (AYP) in reading. Schools that fail to demonstrate AYP for two consecutive years are labeled as needing improvement. Once this happens, schools may have to provide transfers to public schools that have achieved their targeted AYP as well as supplemental services, such as tutoring:

- "In the first year that a school is considered to be in need of improvement, parents receive the option to transfer their child to a higher-performing public school, including a charter school, in the district. Transportation must also be provided" (U. S. Department of Education, 2004, p. 4).
- "In the second year [of needing improvement] . . . the school must continue offering public school choice, and the school must also offer supplemental services (e.g., free tutoring) to low income students" (U. S. Dept. of Education, 2004, p. 5).

This may not be as good as it sounds. First, unlike IDEA services, NCLB transfers and supplemental services (e.g., tutoring) depend on the school's finances, especially federal funding, which is often inadequate. Second, if one school in a district needs improvement, others probably do too. Unfortunately, if a school needing improvement is near an exceptionally good school, too many transfers may turn it from a good school into a "failing" school. Finally, the quality of tutoring may vary tremendously, as tutoring will be provided by a hodgepodge of private, for-profit companies and non-profit organizations. As with much of NCLB, the states have yet to figure out how to monitor and assess the quality of tutoring

Despite the difficulty that many educators and parents have with NCLB (e.g., dependence on standardized tests, inadequate funding), school personnel feel threatened by NCLB—they do not want the newspapers labeling them as "failing," something that can happen if the school as a whole or a subgroup of the school's students does poorly on the state's NCLB tests. Thus, schools feel pressured to remediate reading problems, especially if they're caught early on, when they're easier to remediate. Although this does not give you specific rights unless the school has been legally identified as needing improvement and although NCLB has nothing to do with classifying your child as eligible for special education, NCLB can provide you with psychological and political leverage. To use this leverage, be polite, be respectful, be honest, but if the school denies your child needed services, be assertive: Remind school personnel that your child's poor test scores can hurt everyone, including them—use the NCLB as legitimate leverage.[7]

[7] If your child is classified as eligible for special education under IDEA, you may have additional leverage as states must annually inform the federal government of the progress of students with disabilities. the indicators of progress that states must use are directly linked to NCLB indicators of AYP.

Critical Components of Reading Instruction: A Reading Plan

For your child's reading program to have a good chance of improving her reading, you should meet with school personnel to develop a reading plan (e.g., IEP). At minimum, it should:

- List and describe your child's independent, instructional, and frustration reading levels. As the name infers, children should be instructed with materials at their instructional level; at this level, teachers work directly with students; students easily recognize 95% or more of the words they encounter and understand 70% or more of what they read. At the independent level, children easily recognize 99% of the words they encounter and understand 90% or more of what they read; homework should be at this level. Frustration level materials should be avoided, as they cause emotional distress and block learning; at this level, children stumble with words, recognize fewer than 90% of the words they encounter and understand less than 70% of what they read.
- List and describe your child's specific reading difficulties (e.g., difficulties in quickly recognizing common words, analyzing unknown words, or comprehending grade level materials).
- List and describe the general methods and learning strategies that teachers and reading specialists will initially use to instruct your child.
- List and describe the level, type, and complexity of in-class work and homework assignments likely to frustrate and demoralize your child and the characteristics of assignments likely to make her feel successful and competent.
- List two to four ambitious but realistic reading goals, goals that with quality instruction your child should achieve without frustration (e.g., "By the end of the 4th marking period, Carol will read at a 4th grade instructional level in the XYZ basal series").
- List, for each goal and marking period, an objective or benchmark that clearly indicates whether your child is making "meaningful" progress (e.g., "Carol will read new 3rd grade selections of approximately 250 words, with 98% word recognition accuracy, on three successive occasions, by the end of the 2nd marking period"). Although not generally required by IDEA, objectives or benchmarks linked to marking periods make assessing progress manageable and provide information needed to quickly modify a failing program.
- List the services needed to assure substantial progress in reading (e.g., "Daily, Carol will receive 1-hour of one-to-one tutoring by a reading specialist").

- List and describe the accommodations and modifications needed to assure your child's success in her regular education classes and other instructional settings; this may include short assignments, specialized software, non-stigmatizing textbooks at her independent and instructional levels, in-class support teachers, and modified curricula.
- Describe how the different parts of your child's reading program (e.g., reading instruction in her regular education class and tutoring) will be coordinated so she does not get confused.

Instructional Considerations

To make meaningful progress in reading, struggling readers frequently need counseling, several hours of extra reading help weekly, one-to-one tutoring or small group instruction (two or three students) from a reading specialist, or daily instruction from a reading specialist over the summer. If your child is eligible for special education under IDEA, and if valid, relevant information shows that these or other services are needed to make progress or avoid regression, IDEA requires that schools offer these services, even if they have to create them from scratch.

Pull-out Programs

Many teams of qualified professionals, administrators, teachers, and parents believe that placing children in pull-out resource center programs for part of the day produces adequate progress in reading. Sometimes it does. But sadly, these and other pull-out programs often produce minimal progress, even regression. Four reasons explain this. First, resource center teachers are special education teachers. As such, many lack sufficient education in reading disabilities, which is an extraordinarily complex field. This dramatically reduces their effectiveness, despite good intentions. Second, aides often provide these children with a great deal of pull-out and in-class reading instruction. Even under the direct supervision of teachers, many aides lack the knowledge and skill needed to provide quality instruction—they don't know how to respond to the struggling readers' difficulties. Third, compared to average achieving children, struggling readers need far more relevant reading instruction and opportunities to read materials they find interesting, easy, or moderately challenging. Unfortunately, in resource centers, these children frequently get little relevant instruction and few reading opportunities. And fourth, to avoid confusion and to provide sufficient reinforcement, struggling readers need systematic, integrated, coordinated instruction. Because resource center and regular classroom teachers often have little or no opportunity to regularly observe struggling readers in each others' classes and to jointly plan lessons, these children often get fragmented, uncoordinated, contradictory lessons that confuse and frustrate them. Part of the solution is to write a plan (e.g., an IEP or a Section 504 accommodation plan) that explicitly provides the services of a reading specialist, provides ample opportunity for all instructional staff to observe one another instruct your child, and provides regularly scheduled times to jointly plan lessons.

Reading Specialists

As a parent, you should respectfully insist that your child get whatever extra reading instruction from a reading specialist that she needs and that the specialist meet with your child's regular and special education teachers at least twice a month to coordinate instruction in reading and related areas (e.g., social studies). At a minimum, the professionals teaching your child to read must have training adequate to meet the goals and objectives in her reading plan. Keep in mind that reading is complicated and that reading disabilities is even more complicated. Without coordinated instruction and without monitoring and supervision from a reading specialist, struggling readers are unlikely to succeed in reading. As the American Federation of Teachers (1999) noted, "teaching reading is a job for an expert . . . teaching reading is rocket science" (p. 1).

Parent and Student Support

To better understand your child's educational needs and to learn how to accelerate her learning and help her at home—in ways that avoid conflict and confusion—you might request regular parent training and counseling. Under IDEA, schools can provide these as related services if, as with all related services, you can make a compelling case that these services are necessary for your child "to benefit from special education" (20 U. S. C. §1401, Definition). If the school's IEP Team members agree, list the services and their annual goals in the IEP. Unfortunately, to provide such services, many schools require IDEA eligibility.

Many professionals forget that emotional issues often block students' learning, that often learning success depends on effectively resolving emotional issues. If this happens, share quotes from the professional literature. Here are two:

- When reading is viewed as a threat, children build negative self-schemas of who they are and who they can become. This way of thinking causes a dark mood to envelop their perceptions and they come to believe they are incapable of success. If this mood is persistent, chronic difficulties like learned helplessness may occur. Emotions go beyond the domain of reading to cut at the very soul of a child. (Zambo & Brem, 2004, p. 200)
- Emotional disorders and problems with social development are generally the result, rather than the cause, of learning problems . . . As children with learning problems appraise themselves in relation to others, they often see that they fall short in terms of achievement. They are

> usually members of the low-reading group, and reading—or any academic subject—becomes a stress filled, anxiety producing situation. As a result, these children are more vulnerable to stress and pressures exerted by their environment. They attempt to minimize these pressures by developing varying defense mechanisms. One defense mechanism is withdrawing from participation in classroom activities and social activities; another is to become loud and aggressive, finding ways to be irritating and upsetting. Both of these avoidance techniques serve to mask their fear of failure. By emphasizing one behavior, such as acting out, attention can be distracted from other areas of inadequacy. (Rupley & Blair, 1989, p. 314)

If your child has emotional issues that interfere with academic success or that resulted from reading difficulties, IDEA and Section 504 provide excellent justification for requesting regular counseling. IDEA requires annual goals to "meet the child's needs that *result* from the child's disability . . . [to] meet each of the child's other educational needs that *result* from the child's disability" (20 U.S.C. §1414, Evaluations and IEPs, italics added). Thus, emotional scars from ongoing reading difficulties and adverse emotional reactions to academics (e.g., refusal to read, extreme passivity during reading, disruptive behaviors during academics) merit professional intervention sufficient to meet your child's needs. As with most interventions, they should be focused, planned, systematic, and positive.

To use IDEA, discuss your child's emotional issues with the IEP Team, develop preliminary goals, ask the IEP Team to list counseling as a related service, meet with the counselor to discuss the goals, routinely meet with the counselor to monitor your child's progress and decide how to coordinate efforts, and if necessary, ask the counselor to meet with the IEP team to modify the goals. Although IDEA and Section 504 provide the opportunity to get counseling, you might need to insist that the school provide it frequently enough to ensure success.

Your Child's Progress

Good educational policy, as well as IDEA, require that your child's school inform you of your child's progress. In addition to report card grades and teacher comments, listen to your child read and look at his written work. If you suspect inadequate progress, request a meeting with your child's teacher, a meeting that gives you enough time to fully discuss issues and solve problems. At the meeting, ask the teacher to summarize your child's progress; if it's inadequate, jointly figure out how to accelerate it.

If, after a month, your child continues to make inadequate progress, and under IDEA she is eligible for special education:

- Review your child's program with her teacher and the members of her IEP Team most likely to figure out what's blocking progress.
- Request an evaluation from a reading specialist if the school cannot figure out how to increase your child's rate of progress. Ask that the evaluation include diagnostic teaching and observations of your child in all subjects involving reading and writing. If you were dissatisfied with the previous reading evaluation, ask for an independent evaluation from a university reading clinic or someone with a doctorate in reading disabilities. In the short and long run, it's cheaper for the school to hire an expert who gets to the heart of the matter and identifies solutions than it is to perpetuate failure.
- Ask for a new IEP that provides accommodations, modifications, and services likely to accelerate progress. Make sure that the new program is closely monitored and that all parties agree to meet every four to six weeks to share data documenting progress.

Resolving Disagreements

For legitimate reasons, school personnel may disagree with some of your opinions, observations, and requests. Getting into verbal fights or power struggles to prove that you're right and they're wrong creates resentment, but rarely improves the situation. In most instances, you're likely to achieve satisfactory resolution if you treat school personnel with respect and focus on problem solving. This can be done by:

- Listening to fully understand their concerns and opinions.
- Summarizing their main points.
- Asking them to objectively lay out all major facts on a single piece of paper, in straightforward, non-technical language.
- Asking them to explain their analysis of the major facts.
- Asking them to discuss what they think will produce success in reading.
- Asking them to share the peer-reviewed literature that impartially discusses their recommendations.
- Asking them to join with you in creating clear, short-term objectives or benchmarks to assess progress.
- Asking them what data they will collect to monitor progress.
- Asking them what they recommend doing if, after a month, progress remains poor.

In other words, treat differences as problems to be solved rather than fights to be fought. If this proves unsatisfactory, you may request an independent evaluation, hire a reading specialist to help develop a reading program, or meet with a special education attorney to discuss the pros and cons of initiating an impartial due process hearing.

TAKING ACTION

Being a parent is not easy, especially if your child struggles with reading. Nevertheless, you can do a great deal to help your child succeed in reading if you learn all you can about IDEA, Section 504, NCLB, and reading difficulties. But you must go beyond learning and take action. You must

- Investigate fully your child's learning needs.
- Monitor your child's progress continuously.
- Make informed requests.
- Schedule regular meetings with school personnel to assess data and monitor progress.
- Meet with teachers to coordinate efforts between school and home.
- Treat disagreements as problems to be solved.
- Make sure, if your child is eligible for special education, that her IEP or Section 504 plan is likely to provide her with the instruction and services needed to succeed in reading.

Although there are no guarantees, by taking these steps you dramatically increase the probability that your child will successfully learn to read.

REFERENCES

American Federation of Teachers (1999). *Teaching reading is rocket science.* Retrieved February 27, 2005 from http://www.aft.org/topics/reading/rocket.htm

Individuals with Disabilities Education Act Amendments of 2004 (IDEA), Pub. L. No. 108–446 (2004).

No Child Left Behind Act of 2001, Pub. L. No. 107-110 (January 8, 2002).

Rehabilitation Act of 1973, Pub. L. 93–112 (1973).

Rupley, W. H., & Blair, T. R. (1989). *Reading diagnosis and remediation (*3rd ed.). Columbus, OH: Merrill.

U. S. Department of Education (2004). *No Child Left Behind: A toolkit for teachers.* Washington, D.C.: Author.

Zambo, D., & Brem, K. (2004). Emotion and cognition in students who struggle to read: New insights and ideas. *Reading Psychology, 25,* 189–204.

Howard Margolis, Ed.D., is a Professor of Educational and Community Programs at Queens College of the City University of New York, where he specializes in reading disabilities and special education. He is former editor of the Journal of Educational and Psychological Consultation; currently, he is editor of the Reading & Writing Quarterly: Overcoming Learning Difficulties. (© Howard Margolis, 1067 Pendleton Court, Voorhees, NJ 08043, Voice 856-772-3853, Fax 856-770-8490, E-mail hm08043@yahoo.com)

Insights on Learning Disabilities 2(2), 23–41, 2005

Neurofeedback Treatment of Three Adults with Attention Deficit Hyperactivity Disorder and Related Conditions

Edward H. Jacobs

Londonderry, New Hampshire

Neurofeedback is an operant conditioning biofeedback process that reinforces selective patterns of brain wave activity. The treatment of three adult men with ADHD and related symptomatology is described. Related problems were a nonverbal learning disability, explosive temper, tics, obsessive-compulsive behaviors, and fatigue. Impairments in school and family functioning were evident. Each individual received protocols based on their symptoms and impairments, and were treated twice weekly for 20-minute sessions. Symptoms were identified and tracked with a self-rating scale. Each individual improved in all tracked symptoms, without adverse effects. The findings with adults are consistent with evidence that neurofeedback can improve the functioning of children and adults with ADHD and related problems. The improvement noted is theoretically a function of improved brain self-regulation. This is accomplished without reliance on medication and the concomitant side effects and compliance problems. One patient discontinued his use of medication. Additional research is needed to demonstrate the therapeutic efficacy of neurofeedback for adults in general and with specific disorders.

Neurofeedback is an operant conditioning biofeedback process by which an individual learns to alter the electrical activity of his or her brain through the monitoring of his or her brainwave frequency activity and the rewarding of certain frequency patterns. Also known as brainwave biofeedback or EEG biofeedback, this process seems to help the central nervous system more adaptively regulate attention through enhancing more optimal states of arousal, and inhibiting brain wave activity associated with underaroused and overaroused mental states (Othmer, Othmer, & Kaiser, 1999).

Children with ADHD and learning disabilities have been shown to exhibit abnormalities in their electroencephalographic (EEG) activity (Chabot, Merkin, Wood, Davenport, & Serfontein, 1996; Chabot & Serfontein, 1996; Lazzaro et al., 1998; Mann, Lubar, & Zimmerman, 1992; Matsuura et al., 1993).

Studies have demonstrated that EEG activity could be trained by operant conditioning in humans (Sterman & Friar, 1972, Sterman, MacDonald, & Stone, 1974). Subsequently, neurofeedback training was found to result in changes in brainwave patterns in individuals with ADHD or learning disabilities (Fenger, 1995; Tansey & Brainwave Signatures, 1985; Tansey & Bruner, 1983).

Several clinical and experimental studies have also found that training individuals to alter the electrical activity of the brain decreased symptoms of ADHD (Linden, Habib, & Radojevic, 1996; J. F. Lubar, 1991; J. O. Lubar & Lubar, 1984; Monastra, Monastra, & George, 2002; Othmer, Othmer, & Marks, 1992; Tansey, 1990).

Neurofeedback has also resulted in improvements in different aspects of learning and cognitive functioning (Cunningham & Murphy, 1981; Fenger, 1995; Murphy, Darwin, & Murphy, 1977; Nall, 1973; Whisenant & Murphy, 1977).

Although many of the research and clinical studies have been conducted on children, there have been studies that have indicated an improvement in learning and attention in adults as a result of neurofeedback training (Albert, Andrasik, Moore, & Dunn, 1998; Egner & Gruzelier, 2004; Rasey, Lubar, McIntyre, Zoffuto, & Abbott, 1996; Thompson & Thompson, 1998; Vernon et al., 2003).

This paper will describe the methods and outcomes of neurofeedback treatment with three adult men with ADHD and related conditions.

Method

The three participants were patients in the outpatient psychological services practice of the author. They had been referred to the author by professionals in the community.

The individuals participated in neurofeedback training based on the procedures developed by Othmer et al. (1999). For the majority of the time, these procedures involved simultaneously monitoring three brainwave frequencies, with the subject being rewarded for increasing the amplitude of electrical activity in one of the frequency ranges (the reward band), and for decreasing the amplitude of electrical activity in two of the frequency ranges (the inhibit bands). The frequency ranges were measured in hertz (Hz). A hertz is a unit of frequency of electromagnetic waves wherein one hertz is equal to one cycle per second.

The men were trained to (a) inhibit slow wave activity (in the 2–7 Hz range), in order to decrease distractibility and underaroused mental states; (b) inhibit fast wave activity (in the 22–30 Hz range), in order to decrease overaroused states such as agitation and anxiety; and (c) increase the activity in a middle range (e.g. 10–13 Hz, 11–14 Hz, 12–15 Hz, 15–18 Hz), in order to foster a state of calm, focused attention.

The slower of the two inhibit bands was inhibited approximately 20% of the time (when the microvoltage amplitude was over a set threshold), the faster of the inhibit bands was inhibited approximately 10% of the time (when the microvoltage amplitude was over a set threshold), and the reward band was reinforced approximately 60%–80% of the time (when the microvoltage amplitude was over a set threshold), although there was moment to moment variability, depending on the performance of the individual. The reward and inhibit bands, and the frequency of rewards administered, were individualized for each participant, depending on his clinical picture, and his responses to the training. Thresholds for the inhibit and reward bands were selected by a computer based on the brainwave activity of the individual. These were modifiable throughout the training by signaling the computer to readjust the thresholds when the training either became too easy or too difficult for the person. The electrode placement for each man was also individualized based on the above-mentioned factors.

Feedback was administered by points earned in a video game, the action in which was controlled by the participant's brainwave activity. For each half-second that the individual's brainwave activity was over threshold in the reward band, and below threshold in both of the inhibit bands, the men would earn a point. Each point earned was accompanied by both visual and auditory feedback, which was specific to the game selected by the person.

The visual feedback consisted of seeing the action in the game advance. For example, in the game called Mazes, a black circle turned bright yellow, and advanced through a maze while seeming to devour dots in its path. In a game called Space Race, three space ships were poised in outer space, and points were earned when the middle space ship advanced while the two space ships on either side of it remained stationary. Auditory feedback consisted of audible beeps each time a point was scored.

A second type of protocol was used for one of the participants. This protocol, which trains the brain to increase slow wave activity in the 4–7 Hz and 8–11 Hz ranges in the parietal lobes with eyes closed, is intended to promote a state of deep relaxation in order to counter anxiety and improve the individual's response to stress. The individual sits in a reclining position with his eyes closed, and hears a combination of soothing sounds (i.e. a running brook, breaking waves, a "bing" sound, and a deeper "bong" sound) as rewards for increasing and maintaining electrical activity in the 4–7 Hz and 8–11 Hz frequency ranges.

The equipment used was a two-computer system purchased from NeuroCybernetics, Inc. (21601 Vanowen Street, Suite 100, Canoga Park, CA) using NeuroCybernetics software, versions 3.10 or 3.13f, with a single-channel setup. Three electrodes were used in each training session, with the skin sites cleaned with an alcohol prep pad, and the electrodes connected to the skin with 10–20 conductive paste.

Electrodes were placed on sites on the scalp and the earlobes according to the International 10–20 System of identification, as illustrated in Figure 1.

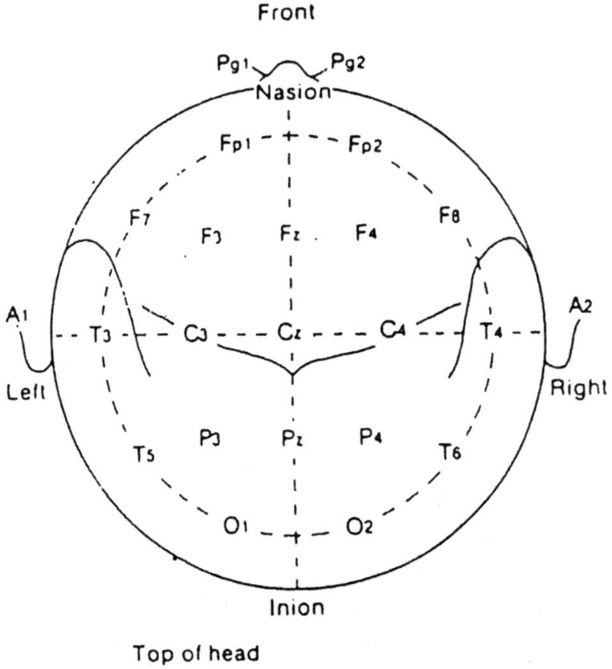

Figure 1. The International 10–20 System of electrode placement

Unipolar placements consisted of one electrode being placed on one side of the scalp, along with a reference electrode clipped to the same side earlobe, and a ground electrode clipped to the opposite side earlobe. In the case of a unipolar electrode being placed along the midline of the scalp, the reference electrode was placed on the left earlobe and the ground electrode was placed on the right earlobe. Bipolar placements, in which two electrodes were placed on the scalp (one as primary, one as reference), and one ground electrode was placed on the earlobe contralateral to the primary electrode, were used when two brain sites were trained simultaneously, and rewards were then based both on high amplitude and differences in phase in the reward band frequency of the two sites. Bipolar placements that included one site from each of the two hemispheres of the brain are referred to as "bihemispheric" placements. The classification system refers to a scalp placement as the primary site (e.g. C4), with the reference electrode (scalp or earlobe placement) as the secondary site (e.g. A2).

Symbollically such placement would be presented as C4 and A2 separated by a minus sign (e.g. C4–A2).

For all participants, target problems were identified by the patient and monitored at each session on the Neurofeedback Progress Chart, a problem tracking form developed by Matthew Fleischman, Ph.D. On the chart, the individuals identified one or more problems that were targeted for improvement through neurofeedback training. Prior to treatment, the men rated the severity of each problem on a 0–4 scale, on the right hand side of the chart, with the following values assigned to the ratings: 0 = Not at all; 1 = Just a little; 2 = Some; 3 = Pretty much; and 4 = Very much. Participants provided ratings again at the beginning of each training session. On the left hand side of the chart was a running list, on each line of which was entered the session number, the date of the training session, and the training protocols used (the sites of the electrode placements and the inhibit and reward frequencies used). The chart was organized in such a way that each session's problem ratings were set alongside—directly to the right—of the training protocol from the previous session, thereby giving information about how the subject had functioned since the last training session, in order to assess whether there might be a correlation between specific training protocols and problem severity.

Participants and Treatments

Participant One: Twenty-Two Year Old Man Diagnosed With ADHD and a Nonverbal Learning Disability

Presenting problems

Seth was a 22 year old young man who was diagnosed with Attention Deficit Hyperactivity Disorder, Predominantly Inattentive Type, and a nonverbal learning disability, with his most severe deficits in the areas of visual-spatial organization and slow processing speed. He had difficulty learning to read in the first and second grades, and received remedial reading instruction. In later elementary school through high school, he had difficulties with math and foreign languages, resulting in occasional failing grades. Seth also suffered from significant anxiety. He had a history of panic attacks dating back to elementary school.

A few months prior to his initial appointment, Seth had left college toward the end of his freshman year, after struggling all year to complete his work. He had great difficulty managing his time and organizing his work, and felt increasingly overwhelmed as he fell further behind during the school year. Seth's impaired attention and visual-spatial processing resulted in several problems in learning. He could not store multiple elements in working memory and, therefore, had difficulty completing multiple-step tasks. He had difficulty retaining grammatical rules and math facts. He struggled in school despite having an IQ that had been measured in the 140s on two occasions, making him intellectually gifted. He was a voracious reader who eagerly consumed complex texts in philosophy, religion, and the arts, and was always eager to discuss his ideas about these subjects with others.

At the time of treatment, Seth was working long hours at a retail store, interacting with customers and helping with some of the managerial tasks. His job required a lot of memorization and long hours. He was living with his parents until he was accepted into another college. Seth's goal was to return to college in order to successfully complete his degree and enter a profession, perhaps in academia.

Treatment

Seth was seen for 34 neurofeedback training sessions lasting for one half hour each and meeting twice weekly. In each session, he spent approximately 20 minutes training on the equipment. If more than one protocol was used during the session, the time was evenly divided between the different protocols. He was not receiving any other form of psychological intervention at the time, nor was he taking medication.

Seth identified the target problems on the problem tracking chart. His pre- and post-neurofeedback ratings on the 0-4 scale are indicated in Table 1.

Table I

Pre- and Post-treatment Ratings of Target Symptoms in the Neurofeedback Treatment of a 22-year Old Man

PROBLEM	PRE-TREATMENT	POST-TREATMENT
Anxiety	4	0
Remembering routine details	4	0
Following through with routine tasks	4	0
Time management	4	0
Organization	4	0

Seth was treated with the protocols presented in Table 2. All protocols, except where indicated, used inhibits of 2-7 Hz and 22-30 Hz.

The designation C3–A1 refers to an electrode placement over the central strip of the left hemisphere, above the preauricular point (the area in front of the ear canal), close to the top of the head, with a reference electrode on the left earlobe, and a ground electrode on the right earlobe. The designation C4-A2 refers to an electrode placement over the central strip of the right hemisphere, above the preauricular point, close to the top of the head, with a reference electrode on the right earlobe, and a ground electrode on the left earlobe. The designation C3–C4 refers to the main electrode being placed in the C3 position, the reference electrode placed in the C4 position, and the ground electrode placed on the right earlobe. The designation CZ–A1 refers to an electrode placement on the top of the head, along the midline which, looking from above, appears to be placed midpoint between the two preauricular points. The reference electrode was on the left earlobe and the ground electrode was on the right earlobe. The designation C3–FP1 refers to the primary electrode being placed at the C3 site with the reference electrode placed over the left pre-frontal lobe of the brain, above the center-right part of the left eyebrow, with the ground electrode placed on the right earlobe. The designation FP1–FP2 refers to the primary electrode being placed on the FP1 site with the reference electrode placed at the contralateral site on the right side, and the ground electrode placed on the right earlobe. The PZ–A1 designation refers to the main electrode being placed in the center of the back of the head, along the midline, with the reference electrode on the left earlobe and the ground on the right earlobe.

Table 2

Electrode Placements and Reward Frequencies, in the Neurofeedback Treatment of a 22–year OldMan

Session #	Protocol 1 electrode placement	Reward frequency range (in Hz)	Protocol 2 electrode placement	Reward frequency range (in Hz)
1–9	C3–A1	15–18	C4–A2	12–15
10–11	C3–C4	11–14		
12–16	CZ–A1	11.5–14.5		
17–18	C3–FP1	11.5–14.5		
19–30	C3–FP1	12–15	FP1–FP2	10–13
31–34	PZ–A1 (eyes closed)	4–7 and 8–11		

Seth began treatment with the C3–A1 and C4–A2 protocols for half of each session. The C3–A1 protocol was used in order to increase the level of arousal by activating the central strip in the left hemisphere of the brain. The goal of this protocol was to increase Seth's arousal level and, therefore, his ability to focus and sustain his attention. The C4–A2 protocol was used in order to increase alertness and, simultaneously, decrease anxiety and enhance calmness.

After six sessions, Seth's mother reported that he seemed calmer and much more focused. He had been remembering his family responsibilities, such as taking care of the cars and shopping for groceries, and following through on multiple-step tasks, better than previously. He was also better at communicating what he had done, so his parents were not left wondering about whether or not Seth had done what his family needed him to do. Seth's mother had noted that she did not need to remind Seth of his responsibilities several times a day, as she had before. Seth was doing better at work, and he had succeeded in memorizing the new inventory items at the store where he worked.

Although Seth was functioning better, he felt that the protocol caused fatigue for several hours after the training. The decision was made to switch the protocol to C3–C4. Seth felt a sharper focus with this protocol, but was still experiencing some fatigue afterwards. We then tried CZ–A1 in order to see if his increased alertness could be maintained without the fatigue; that placement had the desired effect. Shortly after that, we added the protocols C3–FP1 and FP1–FP2 in order to improve executive functions in general, and planning and organization in particular. Different reward band frequency ranges were tried out during the sessions to determine which would give Seth the greatest degree of alertness with the least amount of fatigue.

During this period, Seth reported that he had been following through with more complex tasks, organizing the various sequential steps independently, and remembering to do each one. One such task was planning meals, from deciding what to cook, to making a list of ingredients, buying the items, and preparing and serving the meal. He reported that, prior to the neurofeedback training, he had never been able to accomplish this type of task independently from start to finish. He was able to stay focused on an idea when engaged in conversation with others without getting side-tracked. His mother concurred with these impressions. Seth also wrote his college essays during this period and received an acceptance to a college that specializes in educating bright students with learning disabilities.

Following his acceptance to college, Seth found that his anxiety was increasing in anticipation of beginning another college and potentially failing. We decided to train at PZ with his eyes closed in an alpha/theta training protocol in order to promote relaxation and a greater sense of well-being. After four sessions, Seth reported that he felt "on top of things" mentally, and was looking forward to college with excitement rather than with anxiety.

Throughout the treatment, Seth's ratings reflected a steady improvement in all problem areas, with very few instances of backsliding. By the 28th session, all of the problems that we were tracking were rated as "0" ("Not at all"), and stayed at 0 for the duration of the training.

By the end of treatment, Seth was reporting the following: he felt calm and confident, and had an improved feeling of well-being; he was excited rather than nervous about starting college; he was meeting all of the responsibilities of his job more than satisfactorily; his relationship with his parents was more harmonious, as he was not in conflict with them about meeting his responsibilities and perpetuating communication failures; and his parents were happy with the extra effort he was giving to get things done around the house.

One year following the end of treatment, Seth's mother contacted me to report that Seth had completed his first year of college with As and Bs as his grades, that he was challenged and happy with school, that he was completing his work, and that he was taking no medication. He was experiencing no significant anxiety. He still needed some help from faculty members with his organizational skills.

Discussion

This 22 year old young man with ADHD and a nonverbal learning disability was treated with 34 neurofeedback sessions. Improvement was noted in his functioning in all of the problem areas on the symptom tracking form, which were confirmed in both his verbal reports and those of his mother. He reported improved organizational skills; improved short-term memory; an improved ability to initiate, plan and complete complex, multiple step tasks independently; greatly decreased anxiety; and an improved sense of well-being. After quitting one college, he later applied to and was accepted to a four year college that specializes in educating intelligent students with learning disabilities. One year after enrolling in that school, he was earning As and Bs with no medication.

On the problem tracking form, all five of the problems ("Anxiety," "Remembering routine details," "Following through with routine tasks," "Time management," and "Organization") were rated at the highest degree of severity (4, or "Very much") prior to neurofeedback treatment. At the end of treatment, all problems were rated with a 0 ("Not at all"), indicating a high degree of improvement in all problems for which the patient sought treatment.

Participant Two: Brief Treatment of a 30 Year Old Man With ADHD and Explosive Anger

Presenting problems

Jerry was a 30 year old recently married man who referred himself for neurofeedback training after hearing about the positive outcome that a neighbor's child with ADHD had experienced. Jerry had been diagnosed with ADHD, Combined Type in adulthood, but was never comfortable with the idea of taking medication.

Jerry had gone from high school straight into the military, where he found the regimentation, hierarchy and structure suitable for him. Jerry was a very aggressive individual who always began his assignments with enthusiasm, but who soon became bored and began neglecting details. His work life and personal life were marked by unfinished projects that piled up and created repetitive cycles of stress for him.

Jerry usually related with a calm, thoughtful and intelligent demeanor, which belied an explosive temper which could erupt unpredictably when he was under stress. His temper had already ruined his first marriage, in which he engaged in a few incidents of pushing and shoving his wife. Jerry remembered his father as having a violent temper, which contributed to his parents' divorce when he was a teenager. His paternal uncle had similar difficulty managing his anger, and his older brother barely made it out of high school because of the arguments he would get into with his teachers, and the physical fights he had with his peers.

Jerry had also experienced bouts of immobilizing depression in the past, during which he found it hard to motivate himself to get anything done. He was not currently experiencing depression, however.

Jerry was newly married for the second time. Recently discharged from the military, he wanted to go to college full time and go into a scientifically or technically oriented field. He was concerned for two reasons. He was worried about his poor control over his anger and frustration: that it would jeopardize his new marriage as it had his first, and that it would make it impossible for him to cope with the challenges of college level study. He was also worried that he would be unable to sustain his focus and effort to complete his reading assignments and his papers, and to stay alert for lengthy class periods.

Treatment

Jerry was seen for six neurofeedback training sessions lasting for one half hour each, and meeting twice weekly. In each session, he spent approximately 20 minutes training on the equipment. He was not receiving any other form of psychological intervention at the time, nor was he taking medication.

Jerry identified target problems on the problem tracking chart. His pre- and post-neurofeedback ratings on the 0–4 scale are indicated in Table 3.

Table 3

Pre- and Post-treatment Ratings of Target Symptoms in the Neurofeedback Treatment of a 30- year Old Man

PROBLEM	PRE-TREATMENT	POST-TREATMENT
Attention/Focus	4	2
Procrastination	4	2
Listening skills/Study habits	3	0
Poor motivation	3	1

Jerry was treated with the protocols, presented in Table 4. All protocols, except where indicated, used inhibits of 2–7 Hz and 22–30 Hz.

The T3–A1 designation refers to a main electrode placement over the left temporal lobe, just above the preauricular point of the left ear. The T4–A2 designation refers to the contralateral placement on the right side. These protocols were selected to first target the symptoms of emotional instability, given the temporal lobes' role in emotional regulation. They were intended to help Jerry remain calm in the face of frustration and regulate his emotional highs and lows, taking the "edge" off of the more extreme experiences of depression and agitation when they occurred. With greater emotional control, he would have more of an opportunity to pause before acting when he experienced a strong emotional reaction.

Table 4

Electrode Placements and Reward Frequencies in the Neurofeedback Treatment of a 30-year Old Man

Session #	Protocol 1 electrode placement	Reward frequency range (in Hz)	Protocol 2 electrode placement	Reward frequency range (in Hz)
1-6	T3–A1	15–18	T4–A2	12–15

When Jerry came in for his second neurofeedback session, he reported that soon after the first session, he experienced the sharpest attentional focus that he had ever experienced in his life. He felt that his vision was sharper and everything seemed more colorful and distinct. He was listening in class and retaining more than he had anticipated. That sharpness of focus had lasted for the three days between sessions.

Following the third session, Jerry reported that he had studied for a Chemistry exam, and his approach to the material was well organized and thorough. He reported that he had never experienced this much confidence in his mastery of the material going into an exam before. When he took the exam, he felt that he had studied the right material rather than wasting his time on extraneous or less relevant material, as had been his experience in the past.

After the fifth session, Jerry reported that he had been feeling relaxed and calm, and in control both emotionally and physically, consistently since the first session. He felt that he had made more progress more quickly than he had anticipated, and that the benefits had persisted. He decided to end treatment at the sixth session.

Throughout the treatment, the target problems were rated by Jerry prior to each session. The end results are reported in Table 3, but throughout this brief treatment, the ratings reflected a steady improvement.

Discussion

This 30 year old man with ADHD, explosive anger, and a history of depression, was treated with six neurofeedback sessions. Improvements were noted in all four problem areas that were identified on a symptom tracking form. Two of the problem areas ("Attention/Focus" and "Procrastination") had been rated at the highest level of severity (4, or "Very much") initially. Both were rated two levels lower (2, or "Some") at the end of six sessions of treatment. The two other problem areas had been rated at the second highest level of severity (3, or "Pretty much"). At the end of treatment, "Listening skills" was rated with a 0, or as occurring "Not at all," and "Poor motivation" was rated with a 1, or as occurring "Just a little." There was an improvement of all symptoms over time.

Jerry reported a steady sharpness of focus, an ability to study and attend in class to a degree that he had never previously experienced, and a sense of calm and a feeling of well-being that had eluded him in the past.

Participant Three: Forty-Four Year Old Man With ADHD, Tics, Obsessive-Compulsive Symptoms and Fatigue

Presenting problems

Arnold was a 44 year old lawyer whose friends and wife had suggested that he be evaluated for ADHD. Arnold was aware that he often had problems listening to others when he was tired, but he attributed that to being fatigued due to his practice of taking on too much work and getting too little sleep. Arnold was self-employed, and it was difficult for him to set limits on the amount of work that he agreed to take on. Although he functioned on a very high level professionally, he was usually highly stressed, needing to do too much work in too little time. This left Arnold taking home a lot of work. He worked late into the night, and worked at home on weekends, cutting into his ability to relax with his wife and children. Although he made spending time with his children and participating in their activities a priority, Arnold was usually tired and irritable, and he often reacted to his wife and children with annoyance. Arnold's wife complained that often, when he came home from work, which was frequently after a long, intense day, she could not converse with him about family matters as he looked around the room and would not focus on her. Arnold's friends often observed the same thing when they talked to him. His eyes were frequently scanning the environment, and they were often unsure about whether he was listening.

As Arnold detailed his childhood history, he came to recognize a pattern in elementary school of talking out in class, carelessness in his work, and failing to achieve as well as his teachers thought him capable. Furthermore, he had a habit of mentally counting things repeatedly, such as syllables in words, and touching things twice. He had a history of mild tics which he had always attributed to anxiety. His tics included sniffing and tensing the muscles in his chest and sides, especially when he was under stress, which was often. These latter tics could become painful by the end of the day. Arnold also suffered from mild to extreme fatigue most of the time. He woke up tired and had difficulty maintaining his alertness throughout the day. He accomplished all that he did through sheer effort of will. At the end of the day, he was often so fatigued that he felt a nonspecific, generalized feeling of depression and emotional depletion.

Arnold was prescribed Paxil, and his dosage had been gradually increased to 40 mg at the time that he presented for neurofeedback training. Although the Paxil improved his mood and decreased his irritability and tics, it increased his fatigue in the middle of the day.

Treatment

Arnold was seen for 55 neurofeedback training sessions lasting for one half hour each, and meeting twice weekly. In each session, he spent approximately 20 minutes training on the equipment. If more than one protocol was used during the session, the time was evenly divided between the different protocols. He was not receiving any other form of psychological intervention at the time, but he was taking Paxil 40 mg per day.

Arnold identified target problems on the problem tracking chart. His pre- and post-neurofeedback ratings on the 0–4 scale are indicated in Table 5.

Table 5

Pre- and Post-treatment Ratings of Target Symptoms in the Neurofeedback Treatment of a 44-year Old Man

PROBLEM	PRE-TREATMENT	POST-TREATMENT
Attention/Focus	3	1
Fatigue	3	0
Tics	3	1
Irritability	3	1
Obsessive-Compulsive Symptoms	3	2

Arnold presented with a mixture of symptoms of underarousal and overarousal. His fatigue, mood depression and irritability, and inattentiveness were indications of an underaroused nervous system. His tics and obsessive-compulsive symptoms, however, suggested some overarousal or an unstable arousal pattern. His tics and obsessive-compulsive symptoms seemed to increase when he was tired, and also when he was anxious. He also noticed this when he drank wine, which also made him sleepy. Therefore, his tics and obsessive-compulsive symptoms seemed related to his pattern of underarousal but could have also been related to an unstable arousal pattern given their exacerbation when he was anxious.

Treatment

Arnold was treated with the protocols, presented in Table 6. All protocols, except where indicated, used inhibits of 2–7 Hz and 22–30 Hz.

Table 6

Electrode Placements and Reward Frequencies in the Neurofeedback Treatment of a 44-year Old Man

Session #	Protocol 1 electrode placement	Reward frequency range (in Hz)	Protocol 2 electrode placement	Reward frequency range (in Hz)
1	C3–A1	15–18		
2–40	C3–A1	15–18	C4–A2	12–15
41	C3–C4	12–15		
42–45	C3–C4	11.5–14.5		
45–55	C4–P4	11–14		

The C4–P4 designation refers to a main electrode placement on the C4 site, as described previously, with the reference electrode placed to the right side of the center of the back of the head on the same circumferential plane. The ground electrode was placed on the left ear lobe.

The initial protocol was intended to increase alertness and attention by increasing Arnold's general level of arousal. A few hours after the first session, Arnold was suddenly aware that his attention was unusually sharp. He felt sharply focused and aware of his surroundings, very awake and alive, without feeling any increase in anxiety or agitation. Arnold had difficulty sleeping that night. He felt hyper alert. Although he was worried the next day that he had not gotten sufficient sleep, he was alert all day at work and found that, for the first time in years, he did not need coffee to get alert or stay alert.

Arnold came in the day after his first session, and we decided to add right sided training to the left hemisphere training that we had done the previous day. This appeared to ameliorate the insomnia effects without diminishing the increased alertness.

Throughout this initial protocol combination, left sided training combined with right sided training, Arnold's mood steadily brightened. He began to come home from work humming or singing, with energy that he had not previously known. He was able to attend to his wife's conversation in the evening without being distracted by internal or external distractions. He was more relaxed and less irritable, and coped with the daily demands of family life with greater calmness and flexibility.

We decided to try training both hemispheres together (C3–C4) in order to see if we could decrease Arnold's tendency to worry excessively. At first, the protocol seemed to lower Arnold's threshold for anxiety. Worried thoughts were triggered by slightly less intense stimulation than before. The reward frequency range was lowered slightly, and Arnold responded with less worry and greater calmness. He was less preoccupied at night with what he had not accomplished during the day, and with worries about how he would cope with the next day when so many responsibilities had piled up. Arnold also found that the frequency and intensity of his tics decreased.

The protocol C4–P4 was initiated to see if we could have a greater effect on Arnold's tics. The frequency and intensity of all of Arnold's tics decreased. These included mild facial and vocal tics as well as the muscle tensing in his torso. He was no longer going to bed in pain because of the muscle tension in his sides.

One unexpected benefit of having more energy after doing neurofeedback training was that Arnold, for the first time in 20 years, had the energy to exercise and the motivation to control his eating. He began to wake up early in the morning and jog, or walk on his treadmill in the evening after dinner, whereas previously he had been too fatigued. He not only had the motivation to maintain sensible eating habits, but he could withstand not feeling full without feeling deprived. He was able to lose a significant amount of weight and keep it off.

Arnold continued to do well a year after ending neurofeedback treatment. His inattentiveness, tics, irritability, fatigue and obsessive-compulsive symptoms were markedly reduced. During times of heavy stress, his tics, irritability and low mood would increase, but they never achieved the degree of intensity that they previously had. His fatigue tended to vary, but he was able to function during periods of decreased sleep better than he had been able to before treatment. What was particularly pleasing to Arnold was the fact that he was able to gradually decrease his use of Paxil until it was discontinued altogether. Discontinuation of Paxil resulted in a slight increase in tics, obsessive-compulsive symptoms and irritability, but these symptoms were still greatly reduced from what they once had been.

Throughout the treatment, the target problems were rated by Arnold prior to each session. The end results are reported in Table 5, but throughout his treatment, his ratings reflected a steady improvement.

Discussion

This 44 year old man with ADHD, Predominantly Inattentive Type, tics, obsessive-compulsive symptoms and fatigue was treated with 55 neurofeedback sessions. Improvements were noted in all five problem areas that were identified on a symptom tracking form. All of the problem areas had been rated at the second highest level of severity (3, or "Pretty much") initially. At the end of treatment, one problem, "Fatigue" was rated with a 0, or as occurring "Not at all," three problems ("Attention/Focus," "Tics," and "Irritability") were rated with a 1 ("Just a little"), at the second lowest level of severity, and one problem, "Obsessive-Compulsive Symptoms," was rated with a 2 ("Some"). There were improvements in all symptoms.

This subject reported that his mood was brighter on a daily basis, that he could work a long day and still have the energy to attend to his wife and children, that he was less fatigued and irritable, that his obsessive-compulsive behaviors and excessive worrying had decreased, and that his various tics had diminished. He was able to discontinue his Paxil medication with very little negative effect.

General Discussion

This paper presents a clinical discussion of the neurofeedback treatment of three adults with ADHD and problems which often co-occur with ADHD.

The 22 year old young man had been diagnosed with ADHD, Predominantly Inattentive Type and a nonverbal learning disability, with severe deficits in visual-spatial organization and processing speed, as well as significant anxiety. In spite of being intellectually gifted, he had a history of academic problems throughout his schooling and he had recently quit college. He received 34 neurofeedback sessions which combined right hemispheric unipolar, left hemispheric unipolar, left hemispheric bipolar, and bihemispheric training, which also included the inhibition of slow and fast wave brainwave activity. He also received alpha/theta or deep states training. By the end of treatment, he was able to follow through on multiple-step tasks and was more often taking the initiative to plan and organize activities. He was more alert and less fatigued. He was calmer and more confident. He returned to college and was earning As and Bs a year after his training. He also was not experiencing any significant anxiety.

The 30 year old man had been diagnosed with ADHD, Combined Type, and had an explosive temper. He typically approached new challenges aggressively and with enthusiasm, but quickly became bored and neglectful. His explosive temper while under stress had ruined his first marriage. Having recently left the military, he had re-married and was planning to attend college. He wanted to make sure that he was able to focus well enough to succeed in college, and that he could control his anger so as not to jeopardize his marriage. He was given six neurofeedback sessions which consisted of unipolar left and right hemispheric temporal lobe training, with the inhibition of slow and fast wave activity. He reported the sharpest attentional focus that he had ever experienced, which began immediately after the first session and lasted throughout the training. He was listening in class, retaining the material, and organizing his studies. He felt calm and in control emotionally, and there had been no loss of control of his anger. Encouraged by his rapid improvement, he decided to end his training after just a brief period.

The 44 year old man with ADHD, Predominantly Inattentive Type, tics, obsessive-compulsive symptoms, and fatigue received 55 neurofeedback sessions which consisted of unipolar left and right hemispheric training, bihemispheric training, and right hemispheric bipolar training, with the inhibition of slow and fast wave activity. His attention and focus improved, his multiple tics decreased, his worrying and his obsessive-compulsive behaviors decreased, and his mood was brighter with a concomitant increase in energy and decrease in irritability and fatigue. He was able to discontinue his antidepressant medication.

The significant changes in these three men were likely caused by improved self-regulation of the central nervous system of each, as articulated in the model proposed by Othmer, Othmer, and Kaiser (1999). Symptoms which had seriously impaired their functioning showed substantial improvement with neurofeedback training, without any reported adverse side effects.

Further research is needed to demonstrate the efficacy of neurofeedback with adults with various diagnoses and symptoms, and to investigate the efficacy of specific protocols for specific types of patients. The clinical effectiveness demonstrated here as well as in other reports, with the lack of reported adverse effects, and the fact that the technique involves no medication or invasive procedures, makes neurofeedback treatment an important subject for investigation.

References

Albert, A. O., Andrasik, F., Moore, J. L., & Dunn, B. R. (1998). Theta/beta training for attention, concentration and memory improvement in the geriatric population. *Applied Physiology and Biofeedback, 23* (2), 109.

Chabot, R. J., Merkin, H., Wood, L. M., Davenport, T. L., & Serfontein, G. (1996). Sensitivity and specificity of QEEG in children with attention deficit or specific developmental learning disorders. *Clinical Encephalography, 27,* 26–34.

Chabot, R. J., & Serfontein, G. (1996). Quantitative electroencephalographic profiles of children with attention deficit disorder. *Biological Psychiatry, 40,* 951–963.

Cunningham, M., & Murphy, P. (1981). The effects of bilateral EEG biofeedback on verbal, visual-spatial, and creative skills in learning disabled male adolescents. *Journal of Learning Disabilities, 14*(4), 204–208.

Egner, T., & Gruzelier, J. H. (2004). EEG biofeedback of low beta band components: Frequency-specific effects on variables of attention and event-related brain potentials. *Clinical Neurophysiology, 115*(1), 131–139.

Fenger, T. N. (1995). *Visual-motor integration and its relation to EEG neurofeedback brain wave patterns, reading, spelling, and arithmetic achievement in attention deficit disorders and learning disabled students.* Paper presented at the meeting of the Society for the Study of Neuronal Regulation, Scottsdale, AZ.

Lazzaro, I., Gordon, E., Whitmont, S., Plahn, M., Li, W., Clarke, S., et al. (1998). Quantified EEG activity in adolescent attention deficit hyperactivity disorder. *Clinical Electroencephalography, 29,* 27–42.

Linden, M., Habib, T., & Radojevic, V. (1996). A controlled study of the effects of EEG biofeedback on cognition and behavior of children with attention deficit disorders and learning disabilities. *Biofeedback and Self-Regulation, 21*(1), 35–49.

Lubar, J. F. (1991). Discourse on the development of EEG diagnostics and biofeedback for attention deficit/hyperactivity disorders. *Biofeedback and Self-Regulation, 16,* 201–225.

Lubar, J. O., & Lubar, J. F. (1984). Electroencephalographic biofeedback of smr and beta for treatment of attention deficit disorders in a clinical setting. *Biofeedback and Self-Regulation, 9*(1), 1–23.

Mann, C. A., Lubar, J. F., & Zimmerman, A. W. (1992). Quantitative analysis of EEG in boys with attention deficit-hyperactivity disorder: Controlled study with clinical implications. *Pediatric Neurology, 8,* 30–36.

Matsuura, M. Okubo, Y, Toru, M., Kojima, T., He, Y., Hou, Y., et al. (1993). A cross-national EEG study of children with emotional and behavioral problems: A WHO: A collaborative study in the Western Pacific region. *Biological Psychiatry, 34,* 59–65.

Monastra, V. J., Monastra, D. M., & George, S. (2002). The effects of stimulant therapy, EEG biofeedback, and parenting style on the primary symptoms of attention-deficit/hyperactivity disorder. *Applied Psychophysiology and Biofeedback, 27*(4), 231–249.

Murphy, P., Darwin, J., & Murphy, D. (1977). EEG biofeedback training for cerebral dysfunction: A research program with learning disabled adolescents. *Biofeedback and Self-Regulation, 2,* 288.

Nall, A. (1973). Alpha training and the hyperkinetic child: Is it effective? *Academic Therapy, 9*(1), 5–19.

Othmer, S., Othmer, S. F., & Kaiser, D. A. (1999). EEG biofeedback: Training for AD/HD and related disruptive behavior disorders. In J. A. Incorvaia, B. S. Mark-Goldstein, & D. Tessmer (Eds.), *Understanding, diagnosing, and treating AD/HD in children and adolescents: An integrative approach* (pp. 235–296). Northvale, NJ: Jason Aronson.

Othmer, S., Othmer, S. F., & Marks, C. (1992). EEG biofeedback training for attention deficit disorder, specific learning disabilities, and associated conduct problems. *Journal of the Biofeedback Society of California,* Fall/Winter, 24–27.

Rasey, H. W., Lubar, J. E., McIntyre, A., Zoffuto, A. C., & Abbott, P. L. (1996). EEG biofeedback for the enhancement of attentional processing in normal college students. *Journal of Neurotherapy, 1*(3), 15–21.

Sterman, M. B. & Friar, L. (1972). Suppression of seizures in epileptic following sensorimotor EEG feedback training. *Electroencephalography and Clinical Neurophysiology 33,* 89–95.

Sterman, M. B., MacDonald, L. R., & Stone, R. K. (1974). Biofeedback training of the sensorimotor electroencephalogram rhythm in man: Effects on epilepsy. *Epilepsia, 15*(3), 395–416.

Tansey, M. A. (1990). Righting the rhythms of reason. EEG biofeedback training as a therapeutic modality in a clinical office setting. *Medical Psychotherapy, 3,* 57–68.

Tansey, M. A., & Brainwave Signatures (1985). An index reflective of the brain's functional neuroanatomy: Further findings on the effect of EEG sensorimotor rhythm feedback training on the neurologic precursors of learning disabilities. *International Journal of Psychophysiology, 4,* 91–97.

Tansey, M. A., & Bruner, R. L. (1983). EMG and EEG biofeedback training in the treatment of a 10-year-old hyperactive boy with a developmental reading disorder. *Biofeedback and Self-Regulation, 8,* 25–37.

Thompson, L. & Thompson, M. (1998). Neurofeedback combined with training in metacognitive strategies: Effectiveness in students with ADD. *Applied Physiology and Biofeedback, 24* (4), 243–263.

Vernon, D., Egner, T., Cooper, N., Compton, T, Neilands, C., Sheri, A., et al. (2003). The effect of training distinct neurofeedback protocols on aspects of cognitive performance. *International Journal of Psychophysiology, 47,* 75–85.

Whisenant, W., & Murphy, P. (1977). Bilateral EEG biofeedback and creativity. *Biofeedback and Self-Regulation, 2,* 322.

Author Notes

Correspondence concerning this article should be addressed to: Edward H. Jacobs, Ph.D., 12 Parmenter Road, Londonderry, New Hampshire 03053. Email: EHJPsych@aol.com

The case studies herein contain composite information and changes in identifying information in order to protect the privacy of the patients.

The Neurofeedback Progress Chart was developed by Matthew Fleischmann, Ph.D., 915 Oak Street #300, Eugene, Oregon 97401.

Insights on Learning Disabilities 2(2), 42–58, 2005

Naturalistic Language Teaching Procedures for Children at Risk for Language Delays

Pete Peterson, Ph.D.
Johnson County Community College

Delays in language acquisition are one of the most prevalent disabilities in early childhood. It has been documented that 70% of 3-to-5-year old children with developmental disabilities have language delays (Wetherby & Prizant, 1992). Delays in language acquisition can have serious deleterious effects on the educational and social development of children (Goldstein & Kaczmarek, 1992; Ramey & Campbell, 1992; Warren & Kaiser, 1986). Children with developmental disabilities are known to be especially vulnerable to environmental conditions that may inhibit language acquisition (Tannock & Girolametto, 1992). Thus, the caregiver is viewed as having a "critical influence on the child and the child's language learning environment" (Hemmeter & Kaiser, 1990, p. 335). Some key interaction variables include the caregiver's responsiveness to child vocalizations, reciprocity in verbal interaction between caregiver and child, frequency of verbal interaction, and the availability of stimulating materials (Bradley & Caldwell, 1976; Hart & Risley, 1992; Huttonlocher, Haight, Bryk, Seltzer, & Lyons, 1991). For example, Hart and Risley (1995) found that the quantity and quality of talk directed toward children as well as parental responsiveness, feedback tone, and guidance style during the first three years of life were positively correlated with beneficial child language outcomes.

To address this need for language intervention in the child's natural settings, including the classroom and home, a number of related language teaching procedures have been developed. These include incidental teaching (e.g., Hart & Risley, 1975), mand-modeling (e.g., Rogers-Warren & Warren, 1980; Warren, McQuarter, & Rogers-Warren, 1984), and time-delay (e.g., Halle, Marshall, & Spradlin, 1979). Taken together, these procedures might be termed naturalistic teaching. Naturalistic language teaching approaches have been increasingly viewed as the treatment of choice for children at-risk or children with developmental disabilities (Noonan & McCormick, 1993; Tannock & Girolametto, 1992).

Naturalistic Language Teaching Procedures

Incidental Teaching

Incidental teaching (Hart & Risley, 1968, 1974) involves the use of naturally occurring situations and the child's interests to facilitate language learning.

Hart and Risley (1975) characterized incidental teaching as "the interaction between an adult and a single child, which arises naturally in an unstructured situation such as free-play and which is used by an adult to transmit information or give the child practice in developing a skill" (p.411). In this approach, the teacher or caregiver takes advantage of naturally occurring teaching situations to provide language-learning opportunities for the child. The situation or activity is "child selected" (Hart & Risley, 1975, p. 412), with the teacher or caregiver following the child's lead or interest.

Once a teacher identifies naturally occurring situations in which a child expresses interest, she or he then uses a series of graduated prompts to encourage the child's responses (Hart & Risley, 1974, 1975). Hart and Risley (1974) identified four levels of prompts associated with incidental teaching. The level of response is dependent on the child's response. A Level 1 prompt involved instituting a 30-second delay when the child displayed an interest in a specific object or material. At Level 2, the teacher prompted the child to ask for the desired object. At Level 3, prompts involved a more elaborate request by the teacher (e.g., the teacher showed the child the toy and asked "what is this?"). Finally, at Level 4, the correct response was modeled by the teacher and the child prompted to imitate the response. Teachers were taught to use the lowest level of prompt that would encourage the correct response by the child.

In one of the first studies of incidental teaching procedures, Hart and Risley (1968) successfully increased preschool children's use of adjective-noun combinations (e.g., red truck). Children were taught these combinations in a structured group setting. Although children increased their use of adjective-noun combinations in the structured settings, the behavior did not generalize to free play settings. To increase the "spontaneous" use of adjective-noun combinations in free play settings access to desired classroom materials (e.g., paints) was made contingent on the appropriate use of these combinations. Teachers used graduated levels of prompts similar to those described above to shape the children's verbal behavior.

Incidental teaching procedures have also been used to shape children's use of compound sentences (Hart & Risley, 1974, 1975). In these studies children were progressively required to increase the complexity of their statements. At first, children were required not only to name the object but also to describe how they would use that object (a compound sentence). Children participating in the studies increased their use of nouns, adjective-noun combinations, and compound sentences.

Mand-Model

The mand-model procedure (e.g., Rogers-Warren & Warren, 1980; Warren et al., 1984) is an extension of the incidental teaching model (essentially prompt levels 2, 3, and 4 of Hart and Risley, 1974). The mand-model procedure involves the teacher manding and/or modeling a response from the child. A mand is a request for a verbal response from the child (e.g., "Tell me what you want" or "Use your words"). If the child responds correctly, the teacher or caregiver praises the child and provides the object of interest. In modeling, sometimes known as child-cued modeling (Alpert & Kaiser, 1992; Kaiser, 1993), the teacher observes the focus of the child's interest (e.g., a toy fire truck) and models the correct verbalization (e.g., "That's a fire truck"). If the child makes the correct verbal response (e.g., "Fire truck"), the teacher then praises the child and provides the object of interest.

The mand-model procedure combines the mand and modeling procedures. In this procedure, the teacher observes the focus of the child's interest (e.g., the toy fire truck) and mands a response from the child (e.g., "Tell me what you want"). If the child makes an incorrect response (e.g., "Choo choo train"), the teacher then models the correct response (e.g, "Say fire truck").

Rogers-Warren and Warren (1980) successfully trained teachers to use the mand-model procedure along with contingent praise. The children participating in the study increased their rates of verbalization in general, as well as their rates of novel words and novel word combinations. Similarly, Warren et al. (1984) demonstrated the effectiveness of the mand-model procedure in promoting generalization across settings and maintenance over time by gradually fading the use of this procedure.

One difference between incidental teaching (e.g., Hart & Risley, 1975) and the mand-model procedure is that incidental teaching is more dependent upon the child's initiations. With the mand-model procedure, the teacher more directly controls the number of opportunities for the child to engage in the language interaction (Rogers-Warren & Warren, 1980). The procedure may be useful, then, for children with very low rates of initiation (Rogers-Warren & Warren; Warren et al., 1984).

Time-Delay

Another extension of incidental teaching is the time-delay or delayed prompt procedure (e.g., Halle, Baer, & Spradling, 1981). Time-delay has been defined as "nonvocal cues for vocal language" (Halle et al., p. 390). In the time-delay procedure, the teacher identifies a situation in which the child wants an object or assistance and then waits for the child to make a response. If this is unsuccessful, the teacher will then use the mand-model procedure. The time-delay procedure is especially useful for teaching children to initiate verbal interaction (Noonan & McCormick, 1993).

Halle, Marshall, and Spradlin (1979) used a time-delay procedure to increase children's "opportunity to respond" for two groups of institutionalized children. Initially, meal trays were withheld for 15 seconds. Of the first set of three children participating in the study, only one appropriately requested the meal tray. Next, modeling of the correct response was added to the delay resulting in an increase in appropriate responding. A second group of three children, who had observed the contingencies implemented for the first three, then participated in the delay condition. These children acquired the requesting behavior and generalized across meal settings and servers.

Charlop, Schriebman, and Thibodeau (1985) used a time-delay procedure to increase spontaneous speech in seven young boys with autism. Pretests were given to determine if each child could label certain preferred items and training was provided if the child did not have these skills in his repertoire. Next, training was provided in which the teacher modeled the correct response (e.g., "I want cookie"). The child would receive the item if he correctly imitated the response. Then a brief time-delay was introduced with delays beginning at two seconds. These were then systematically increased to 10 seconds. All children participating in the study, except one, acquired the target behavior.

Milieu Language Teaching

Incidental teaching, the mand-model procedure, and the time-delay technique have been combined with other strategies to encourage child language in natural environments (Alpert & Kaiser, 1992; Hart & Rogers-Warren, 1978). Hart and Rogers-Warren termed this approach "milieu language teaching." Kaiser (1993) defined milieu language teaching as "a naturalistic, conversation-based teaching procedure in which the child's interest in the environment is used as a basis for eliciting elaborated child communicative responses" (p. 77). Hemmeter and Kaiser (1994) later proposed "enhanced milieu teaching" as a more comprehensive approach to naturalistic language intervention. There are three components to this intervention model: (a) environmental arrangement, (b) responsive interaction techniques, and (c) milieu teaching procedures.

Environmental arrangement involves the arrangement of the child's environment to facilitate language teaching. The goal is to increase the child's engagement with the environment (Kaiser, 1993), while setting up situations in which the child is more likely to use language. For example, having toys or other objects of interest available will make it more likely that the teacher can use the situation to have the child verbalize a request for that toy or object (see Ostrosky & Kaiser, 1991). Another important part of environmental arrangement is to provide an "optimal affective environment for the child" (Kaiser, 1993, p. 76); that is, to keep the interaction nurturing and reinforcing for the child.

Responsive interaction techniques are designed to increase conversational interaction between teacher and child. These techniques include following the child's lead in terms of focus of interest, turn-taking, providing descriptive statements, imitating the child's verbalizations, and expanding on verbalizations made by the child (Kaiser, 1993). Milieu teaching procedures include modeling, mand-modeling, and time-delay. Each of these procedures builds upon the previous one, with later procedures incorporating components of earlier ones (Alpert & Kaiser, 1992), much like Hart and Risely's (1974) incidental teaching.

Effectiveness of Naturalistic Teaching

While little research has been conducted on the effectiveness of naturalistic teaching for children designated as having learning disabilities per se, it has been found to be effective for children from low-income families (e.g., Hart & Risley, 1975, 1980), children with mental retardation (e.g., Gobbi, Cipani, Hudson, & Lapenta-Neudeck, 1986; Warren, 1992), children with developmental delays (e.g., Angelo & Goldstein, 1990, Oswald, Lignugaris/Kraft, & West, 1990), children with language delays (e.g., Rogers-Warren & Warren, 1980; Warren et al., 1984), children prenatally exposed to drugs and in multiple risk families (Peterson, Carta, & Greenwood, 2005), and children with autism (e.g., Charlop et al., 1985; Hancock & Kaiser, 2002; Laski, Charlop, & Schriebman, 1988). Given the range of children for whom this approach is effective it would seem that it would also be useful in teaching children with learning disabilities.

Studies have demonstrated that children were able to acquire and generalize across a range of language targets, including single words (e.g., Charlop et al., 1985; Warren & Gazdag, 1990), combinations (e.g., Cavallaro & Bambara, 1982; Warren & Bambara, 1989), complexity of sentences (e.g., Hart & Risley, 1980), initiations and requests (e.g., Angelo & Goldestein, 1990; Warren et al., 1984; Warren, Yoder, Gazdag, Kim, & Jones, 1993), signing (e.g., Carr & Kologinsky, 1983; Kaczmarek, Hepting, & Dzubak, 1996), reading (e.g, Fabry, Mayhew, & Hanson, 1984), and receptive language (e.g., McGee, Krantz, Mason, & McClannahan, 1983; McGee, Krantz, & McClannahan, 1986).

Naturalistic Teaching vs. Traditional Language Intervention

Naturalistic language teaching has been compared to more traditional, therapist-directed approaches to language intervention, such as discrete trial training (Fey, 1986; Spradlin & Siegel, 1982; Sundberg & Partington, 1998). Discrete trial training is conducted under highly structured conditions in which the therapist selects the stimulus items to be used during the teaching sessions, divides the language target skills into a series of independent tasks, presents these tasks in a series of massed trials until criterion is met, and provides the child an often arbitrary reinforcer combined with praise (Sundberg & Partington, pp. 224–256). In contrast, naturalistic teaching is considered "looser" (Sundberg & Partington), with less emphasis, at least initially, on the correctness of the child's response. This approach follows the child's lead in terms of the stimulus of interest and provides a "natural reinforcer" (usually the object of interest to the child). The reinforcers delivered in naturalistic teaching are considered to be be more functional in relation to the child's response than in the discrete trial training approach.

In the traditional therapist-directed approach (i.e., discrete trial training), language intervention is typically conducted in a speech therapy room and is highly structured by the therapist (Fey, 1986; Sundberg & Partington, 1998). Naturalistic teaching approaches typically work with the child in his or her natural setting (i.e., classroom or home) and usually follow the child's lead or interest, not in terms of the language skill being taught, but in relation to toys and other objects of interest to the child. This requires the teacher to respond more flexibly to naturally occurring language teaching opportunities as they occur throughout the day. The teacher must also be able to identify potential reinforcing contingencies that will be functional for the child in other settings (D. Baer, personal communication, May 30, 1996).

Naturalistic teaching procedures are advantageous in that the teacher or parent has far more opportunities throughout the day to engage in naturalistic teaching than would a speech therapist in a traditional pull-out program (Fey, 1986). Ideally, the use of naturalistic teaching procedures would become "automatic" to the teacher or parent and be used naturally throughout the day. Perhaps the most difficult part of this approach is teaching parents and teachers how to identify naturally occurring opportunities for language interaction.

A number of studies have compared naturalistic teaching with discrete trial training. Miranda-Linne and Melin (1992) found that although children acquired color adjectives faster through discrete trial training, they were more likely to generalize the new language skills following naturalistic teaching. Similarly, McGee, Krantz, and McClannahan (1985) reported that naturalistic teaching promoted greater generalization of new language skills across people and settings than did a more traditional trainer-directed approach. Seifert and Schwarz (1991) compared incidental teaching and direct instruction techniques and found that incidental teaching promoted great generalization across concepts to untrained concepts. Carr and Kologinsky (1983) initially used discrete trial training to teach signing to three children with autism. They then faded to incidental teaching. The results indicated that discrete trial training was best for training the correct form of the signs and incidental teaching was more likely to promote generalization and maintenance. Finally, Charlop-Christy and Carpenter (2000) compared discrete trial training, incidental teaching, and their modified incidental teaching (a combination of discrete trial training and incidental teaching). They found that their modified incidental teaching procedure was superior to either discrete trial training or incidental teaching alone.

It seems that discrete trial or other more structured, therapist-directed approaches may be necessary for establishing language skills initially but that naturalistic teaching strategies will promote better generalization of those skills.

Naturalistic Teaching and Generalization of Language Skills

Researchers and therapists have been concerned for some time about the poor generalization of children's language skills following traditional speech and language intervention (Fey, 1986, 1988; Guess, Keogh, & Sailor, 1978; Warren, 1988). Fey (1986) has called this a "black mark" on the history of language intervention. Problems in achieving generalization can occur, for example, if the generalization environment is too dissimilar to the training situation (e.g., Hemmeter, Ault, Collins, & Meyer, 1996; McGee, Almeida, Sulzer-Azaroff, & Feldman, 1992) or if the child's newly learned language skills are not reinforced in the generalization environment (e.g., Carr & Kologinsky, 1983; Warren & Bambara, 1989).

Generalization occurs when new skills learned in the teaching environment transfer to other situations without further training in those new environments or situations (Stokes & Baer, 1977). Stokes and Baer identifies a number of methods that have been utilized to promote generalization. Some of these methods include: (a) introduce behaviors that will contact naturally occurring contingencies of reinforcement in the generalization settings, (b) provide a range of examples of the target behavior, (c) vary the training routine enough to provide the child exposure to a wider range of stimuli, or "train loosely," and (d) make it difficult for the child to discriminate the contingencies, possibly through the use of an intermittent schedule of reinforcement.

Naturalistic teaching procedures have a number of common characteristics that make them very effective tools for promoting generalization of the child's newly learned language skills. As listed in Kaiser, Yoder, and Keetz (1992, p. 9) these include: (a) language teaching that follows the child's lead or interest, (b) the use of multiple, naturally occurring examples, (c) explicit prompts for the child's use of language, (d) the use of natural consequences to reinforce the child's verbal behavior, and (e) naturalistic teaching strategies that are embedded in the ongoing interaction between teacher and child.

These common characteristics are compatible with the strategies proposed by Stokes and Baer (1977) for promoting generalization of functional language skills in children (Warren & Kaiser, 1986). Following the child's lead or interest and the use of natural consequences increase the probability that the child's behavior will contact naturally occurring contingencies of reinforcement. The loose structure of this approach makes it more likely that the child will be exposed to multiple exemplars (Laski et al., 1988), including variations in location, position of trainer, time of day and so on (see Baer, 1981). This may prevent the behavior from coming under too narrow a range of stimulus control (Kirby & Bickel, 1988). Similarly, the embedded nature of the ongoing teaching interaction may make some of the contingencies less discriminable, perhaps creating "multiple stimulus control" (Halle et al., 1981). In addition, the fact that training is conducted in natural contexts makes it more likely that stimuli common to a wide range of potential language environments will be present. This would be a case of "programming common stimuli" (Stokes & Baer, 1977). Finally, it may also be that the language skills taught in the naturalistic language teaching approach, as compared to more traditional speech and language therapy, are more functional for the child and more likely to generalize to other settings and persons (Fey, 1986; Guess et al., 1978; Sundberg & Partington, 1998). In a review of the naturalistic teaching literature, Peterson (2005) found that 94% of the studies measuring for generalization effects demonstrated generalization.

Teaching Teachers and Parents To Use Naturalistic Language Teaching Skills

A number of studies have successfully trained teachers (e.g., Halle et al., 1981; Kaiser, Ostrosky, & Alpert, 1993; Warren et al., 1984) and parents (e.g., Alpert & Kaiser, 1992; Hemmeter & Kasier, 1994; Laski et al., 1988; Peterson et al., 2005) to implement naturalistic language teaching strategies. The most common strategies for teaching parents and teachers how to implement naturalistic teaching strategies include didactic presentation, modeling, roleplaying, feedback both during interaction with the child and via videotape (e.g., Alpert & Kaiser; Hester, Kaiser, Alpert, & Whiteman, 1995; Kaiser & Hancock, 2003; Kaiser, Hancock, & Hester, 1998; Kaiser et al., 1993; Peterson et al., 2005). Kaiser and Hancock also had parents keep detailed notes of their naturalistic teaching interaction with their children. Kaiser et al. (1998) trained parents as "co-interventionists" in which the therapist models and coaches the parent while they are both involved in a naturalistic teaching interaction with the child. In addition to direct modeling and coaching, the therapist can provide "functional support" to the parent by facilitating certain tasks (e.g., arranging the environment).

Implementing Naturalistic Teaching In The Classroom And Home

There are three essential ingredients for the successful implementation of naturalistic teaching procedures in the classroom and home. These are (a) sensitivity to the child's interests, (b) strategic arrangement of the teaching

Environmental Arrangement

_____ Are interesting toys and materials available to the child?
_____ Does the teacher respond to teaching opportunities?
_____ Is the teacher aware of the child's immediate interest?
_____ Does the teacher follow the child's lead or interest?
_____ Is the affective environment positive and nurturing?

Use of Responsive Interaction and Milieu Teaching Procedures

Mark each time teacher uses a procedure	Naturalistic Teaching Procedure	Rate per Minute
	Descriptive Statements	
	Imitation	
	Expansions	
	Model	
	Mand	
	Mand-Model	
	Time-Delay	

Figure 1. Naturalistic teaching observation checklist

environment, and (c) appropriate use of naturalistic teaching techniques (i.e., mand-model, time-delay).

Sensitivity to the Child's Interests

The best naturalistic teachers are those who are keenly aware of the child's interests both in general and at the moment. While more of an art than a science, a naturalistic teacher should be able to "read" the contingencies surrounding the child's behavior. The teacher must be able to track the child's changing interests and adjust accordingly. Naturalistic teachers can sense when to push for more and when to back off a little without "giving in" to the child. Knowing when to use specific naturalistic teaching strategies and when to change activities depends, in part, on this sensitivity. Sensitivity can be developed through coaching and experience. In addition, the teacher should keep her or his interaction with the child nurturing, positive, and reinforcing (Kaiser, 1993). The Naturalistic Observation Checklist (Figure 1) is an example of an instrument designed for training teachers and collecting data regarding fidelity of treatment. During a training or assessment opportunity an observer collects data on sensitivity to the child's interests, environmental arrangement, and the use of naturalistic teaching techniques. Data can be expressed as pure frequency count or as rate per minute. Furthermore, an observation system utilizing a computer program with codes for both teacher behavior (e.g., descriptive statements, mand-model) as well as child verbal response (e.g., correct response) could be employed to determine the conditional probabilities of a child's verbal behavior following a specific naturalistic teaching behavior by the teacher (see Peterson et al., 2005). Conditional probability data can be a very useful feedback tool for training naturalistic teachers.

Environmental Arrangement

There are a number of strategies that can be used by the teacher to establish a more effective naturalistic teaching environment. Ostrosky and Kaiser (1991) offer a number of useful recommendations for arranging the teaching environment, including (a) making sure that toys, books, and other items of specific interest to the child are available, (b) putting toys and other interesting items out of reach, (c) not providing enough of something of interest so that the child will ask for more, (d) sabotaging, or "forgetting" an important item in a multi-step task so that the child will have to ask for it, (e) giving the child opportunities to make choices, and (f) arranging situations so that the child has to ask for assistance. Each of these strategies is designed to encourage functional language use by the child by arranging a situation in which the child must initiate a request.

The teaching area should include numerous materials (e.g., toys, books) that one is reasonably certain will be of interest to the child. For example, if the child is interested in jungle animals the teacher should make sure that there are toy jungle animals, books with pictures of jungle animals, and perhaps a jungle animal puzzle present in the teaching area. One should never assume that any particular toy, book, object, or activity will be of interest to an individual child (e.g., "Every child likes dinosaurs!"). Once again, the teacher needs to know the child's interests. These toys, books, and objects can be put out of reach so that the child has to request them. The teacher can then employ time-delay, model, mand, or mand-model procedures to prompt the correct verbal response from the child.

Teachers can also arrange a teaching opportunity by providing only some of what is needed to complete a task or activity (e.g., Ostrosky & Kaiser's, 1991, inadequate portions). Some examples might include providing only a small amount of paint needed for a painting project or only a small portion of a snack, so that the child will have to ask for more. This has the added benefit of "priming the pump" in terms of an introduction of a potential reinforcer in incomplete form. A closely related strategy is "sabotage" (e.g, Ostrosky & Kaiser). Sabotage is often accomplished through teaching the child a sequence of behaviors leading to a common outcome and then withholding materials necessary for completion of one of the behaviors. For example, a child might be taught to make chocolate milk using a glass, spoon, chocolate mix, and milk. Assuming that chocolate milk is a reinforcer for the child, after she has mastered the skill of making chocolate milk, the sequence can be "sabotaged" in that materials for one of the steps is withheld (e.g., the glass). Now the child has to verbally request the glass (or milk, or chocolate mix, etc.) in order to make her chocolate milk. This is also a case of arranging the situation so that the child has to ask for assistance.

Giving children an opportunity to choose is another strategy for establishing opportunities to use naturalistic teaching techniques. Depending upon the the child's abilities, one may have to teach the child to make choices, perhaps by at first giving the child a choice between a highly desired item and a non-desired item, employing time-delay, model, mand, and mand-model as needed. Later, the teacher can work toward giving the child choices of more equal value.

Naturalistic Language Teaching Techniques

At the core of naturalistic teaching are the teaching techniques themselves. Table 1 summarizes naturalistic language teaching techniques including descriptive statements, imitating, expansion, modeling, manding, mand-modeling, and time-delay. These techniques can be skillfully and flexibly combined to encourage children's verbal behavior and should be tailored to each child's language learning needs. For example, if a child has the verbal repertoire to request preferred objects but does not do so, time-delay may be a useful strategy to increase that child's verbal initiations. Another child, however, may not have the verbal repertoire to make requests. Then the mand-model procedure would be more appropriate.

Hart and Risley's (1974) levels of incidental teaching provide a fairly well structured example of how these might be combined for naturalistic teaching. As discussed earlier in this chapter, Hart and Risley recommended that the teacher begin with the lowest level of prompt necessary to encourage the child's verbal response beginning with, perhaps, the Level 1 time-delay. If the child does not respond, the teacher would then prompt the child to ask for the desired object. If the child still does not emit the desired response the teacher would then use a more elaborate response by pointing to the object and asking, "What's this?" If this still does not work, the teacher would then model the correct response and the child would be prompted to imitate the teacher.

For example, a teacher with Michael knows that he very much likes fire trucks and fire fighters. The teacher would already have made sure that there were toy fire trucks, books about fire trucks, and perhaps a fire fighter costume

Table 1
Naturalistic Language Teaching Techniques

Technique	Description
Descriptive Statements	Caregiver makes a statement that describes the child's ongoing activities (e.g., "You're picking up the train"), or some other event in the immediate environment (e.g., the phone rings and teacher says, "The telephone is ringing").
Imitating	Caregiver directly imitates a verbal statement made by the child. For example, child says, "fire truck," mom says, "You're right. That's a fire truck."
Expansion	Caregiver expands on the child's statement. The caregiver responds to the child's utterance by repeating it, but adds syntactic or semantic information to what the child said. For example, child says, "fire truck," mom expands by saying, "That's a big red fire truck."
Model	Caregiver produces a word, phrase or sentence with the intention that the child will imitate the verbal behavior. For example, the caregiver, following the child's lead, observes the child's possible interest and models, "I want the red fire truck." Please note that model is different than descriptive statements in that the caregiver intends for the child to imitate the response.
Mand	Caregiver requests an appropriate response from the child. For example, the child is gesturing toward the toy fire truck and mom says, "Tell me what you want."
Mand-Model	Caregiver combines a mand and model at the same time. For example, the child is still interested in the toy fire truck and mom says, "Michael, say I want the red fire truck."
Time-Delay	Caregiver recognizes a situation in which the child wants an object or assistance and then waits to see if the child emits the correct response. The caregiver may use some form of visual prompt (e.g., holding the toy up) or assume a questioning look (e.g., raised eyebrows) or both. For example, mom notices that the child is interested in the toy fire truck, picks up the truck so that the child can see her holding it and then she simply waits for a response from the child.

Adapted from the Combined Milieu, Responsive-Interactive and Hybrid Language Teacher Code (Alpert, Keefer, & Fischer, 1992) available in the room. The teacher observes that Michael is interested in the toy fire truck that has been placed out of reach. The teacher can tell that Michael is interested because he has been standing in front of the shelf that the toy fire truck is on and looking at the toy for some time. First, the teacher moves near the shelf and looks at Michael with an expectant look (communicating nonverbally, "Tell me what you want"). If Michael says "fire truck," the teacher will provide the toy and might also use an expansion like "the big red fire truck" or "You want the red fire truck." If Michael does not emit the correct response to the time-delay within 30 seconds, the teacher would then prompt him by saying "Tell me what you want." If Michael does not state what he wants verbally the teacher might then prompt him further by manding "What is this?" If Michael says "fire truck," she can then give Michael the toy (and probably use one of the expansions described above). If Michael does not say "fire truck" the teacher will then move to the next level of prompt and first model the correct response, "I want the fire truck," and then prompt Michael by saying, "Say I want the fire truck." If Michael successfully emits the response he can then play with the fire truck. If not, then he does not get to play with the toy. It should be noted, however, that shaping may be required here. If a child is only capable of getting out part of a word, for example "truh" (for fire truck), the teacher will need to start with that and shape close approximations as time goes on (later "truck," then "fff truck," then "fire truck").

In conclusion, naturalistic teaching has been demonstrated to be an effective approach to children's language intervention and may be particularly useful in facilitating the generalization and maintenance of children's language skills following intervention. The skillful combining of sensitivity to the child's interests, thoughtful arrangement of the teaching environment, and flexible use of naturalistic teaching techniques can lead to a positive and productive language interaction between teacher and child.

Acknowledgments

I would like to thank Don Baer, Judith Carta, Joe Delquadri and Charles Greenwood for their helpful comments on earlier versions of this manuscript.

Correspondence concerning this chapter should be addressed to Pete Peterson, Ph.D., Associate Professor of Psychology, Liberal Arts Division, Box 36, Johnson County Community College, 12345 College Blvd., Overland Park, KS 66210. Email: ppetersn@cccc.net

References

Alpert, C. L., & Kaiser, A. P. (1992). Training parents as milieu language teachers. *Journal of Early Intervention, 16,* 31–52.

Angelo, D. H., & Goldstein, H. (1990). Effects of a pragmatic teaching strategy for requesting information by communication board users. *Journal of Speech and Hearing Disorders, 55,* 231–243.

Baer, D. M. (1981). *How to plan for generalization.* Austin, TX: PRO-ED.

Bradley, R., & Caldwell, B. (1976). Early home environment and changes in mental test performance 6 to 36 months. *Developmental Psychology, 12,* 93–97.

Carr, E. G., & Kologinsky, E. (1983). Acquisition of sign language by autistic children II: Spontaneity and generalization effects. *Journal of Applied Behavior Analysis, 16,* 297–314.

Cavallaro, C. C., & Bambara, L. M. (1982). Two strategies for teaching language during free play. *Journal of the Association for Persons with Severe Handicaps, 7,* 80–92.

Charlop, M. E., Schreibman, L., & Thibodeau, M. G. (1985). Increasing spontaneous verbal responding in autistic children using the time-delay procedure. *Journal of Applied Behavior Analysis, 18,* 155–166.

Charlop-Christy, M. H., & Carpenter, M. H. (2000). Modified incidental teaching sessions: A procedure for parents to increase spontaneous speech in their children with autism. *Journal of Positive Behavior Interventions, 2,* 98–112.

Fabry, B. D., Mayhew, G. L., & Hanson, A. (1984). Incidental teaching of mentally retarded students within a token system. *American Journal of Mental Deficiency, 89,* 29–36.

Fey, M. E. (1986). *Language intervention with young children.* Austin, TX: PRO-ED.

Fey, M. E. (1988). Generalization issues facing language interventionists: An introduction. *Language, Speech, and Hearing Services in Schools, 19,* 272–281.

Gobbi, L., Cipani, E., Hudson, C., & Lapenta-Neudeck, R. (1986). Developing spontaneous requesting among children with severe mental retardation. *Mental Retardation, 24,* 357–363.

Goldstein, H., & Kaczmarek, L. (1992). Promoting communicative interaction among children in integrated intervention settings. In S. F. Warren & J. Reichle (Eds.), *Causes and effects in communication and language intervention* (pp. 81–111). Baltimore, MD: Paul H. Brookes.

Guess, D., Keogh, W., & Sailor, W. (1978). Generalization of speech and language behavior. In R. Schiefelbusch (Ed.), *Bases of language intervention.* Baltimore, MD: University Park Press.

Halle, J., Baer, D., & Spradlin, J. (1981). Teachers' generalized use of delay as a stimulus control procedure to increase language use in handicapped children. *Journal of Applied Behavior Analysis, 14,* 389–409.

Halle, J. W., Marshall, A. M., & Spradlin, J. E. (1979). Time delay: A technique to increase language use and generalization in retarded children. *Journal of Applied Behavior Analysis, 12,* 431–439.

Hancock, T. B., & Kaiser, A. P. (2002). The effects of trainer-implemented enhanced milieu teaching on the social communication of children with autism. *Topics in Early Childhood Special Education, 22,* 39–54.

Hart, B. & Risley, T. R. (1980). In vivo language intervention: Unanticipated general effects. *Journal of Applied Behavior Analysis, 13,* 407–432.

Hart, B. & Rogers-Warren, A. (1978). A mileau approach to teaching language. In R. Schiefelbusch (Ed.), *Language Intervention Strategies* (pp. 193–235). Baltimore, MD: University Park Press.

Hart, B. M., & Risley, T. R. (1968). Establishing the use of descriptive adjectives in the spontaneous speech of disadvantaged children. *Journal of Applied Behavior Analysis, 1,* 109–120.

Hart, B. M., & Risley, T. R. (1974). Using preschool materials to modify the language of disadvantaged children. *Journal of Applied Behavior Analysis, 7,* 243–256.

Hart, B. M., & Risley, T. R. (1975). Incidental teaching of language in the preschool. *Journal of Applied Behavior Analysis, 8,* 411–420.

Hart, B. M., & Risley, T. R. (1992). American parenting of language-learning children: Persisting differences in family-child interactions observed in natural home environments. *Developmental Psychology, 28,* 1096–1105.

Hart, B. M., & Risley, T. R. (1995). *Meaningful differences in the everyday experiences of young American children.* Baltimore, MD: Paul H. Brookes.

Hemmeter, M. L., Ault, M. J., Collins, B. C., & Meyer, S. (1996). The effects of teacher-implemented language instruction within free time activities. *Education and Treatment of Children, 13,* 331–346.

Hemmeter, M. L., & Kaiser, A. P. (1990). Environmental influences on children's language: A model and case study. *Education and Treatment of Children, 13,* 331–346.

Hemmeter, M. L., & Kaiser, A. P. (1994). Enhanced milieu teaching: Effects of parent-implemented language intervention. *Journal of Early Intervention, 18,* 269–289.

Hester, P. P., Kaiser, A. P., Alpert, C. L., & Whiteman, B. (1995). The generalized effects of training trainers to teach parents to implement milieu teaching. *Journal of Early Intervention, 20,* 30–51.

Huttonlocher, J., Haight, W., Bryk, A., Seltzer, M., & Lyons, T. (1991). Early vocabulary growth: Relation to language input and gender. *Developmental Psychology, 27,* 236–248.

Kaczmarek, L. A., Hepting, N. H., & Dzubak, M. (1996). Examining the generalization of milieu language objectives in situations requiring listener preparatory behaviors. *Topics in Early Childhood Special Education, 16,* 139–167.

Kaiser, A. P. (1993). Parent-implemented language intervention: An environmental perspective. In A. P. Kaiser & D. B. Gray (Eds.), *Enhancing children's communication: Research foundations for intervention* (pp. 63–84). Baltimore, MD: Paul H. Brookes.

Kaiser, A. P., & Hancock, T. B. (2003). Teaching parents new skills to support their young children's development. *Infants & Young Children, 16,* 9–21.

Kaiser, A. P., Hancock, T. B., & Hester, P. P. (1998). Parents as cointerventionists: Research on applications of naturalistic language teaching procedures. *Infants & Young Children, 10,* 45–55.

Kaiser, A. P., Ostrosky, M. M., & Alpert, C. L. (1993). Training teachers to use environmental arrangement and milieu teaching with non vocal school children. *Journal of the Association for Persons with Severere Handicaps, 18,* 188–199.

Kaiser, A. P., Yoder, P. J., & Keetz, A. (1992). Evaluating milieu teaching. In S. F. Warren & J. Reichle (Eds.), *Causes and effects in communication and language intervention* (pp.9–47). Baltimore, MD: Paul H. Brookes.

Kirby, K. C., & Bickel, W. K. (1988). Toward an explicit analysis of generalization: A stimulus control interpretation. *The Behavior Analyst, 11,* 115–129.

Laski, K. E., Charlop, M. H., & Schreibman, L. (1988). Training parents to use the natural language paradigm to increase their autistic children's speech. *Journal of Applied Behavior Analysis, 21,* 391–400.

McGee, G. G., Almeida, M. C., Sulzer-Azaroff, B., & Feldman, R. S. (1992). Promoting reciprocal interactions via peer incidental teaching. *Journal of Applied Behavior Analysis, 25,* 117–126.

McGee, G. G., Krantz, P. J., Mason, D., & McClannahan, L. E. (1983). A modified incidental-teaching procedure for autistic youth: Acquisition and generalization of receptive object labels. *Journal of Applied Behavior Analysis, 16,* 329–338.

McGee, G. G., Krantz, P. J., & McClannahan, L. E. (1985). The facilitative effects of incidental teaching on preposition use by autistic children. *Journal of Applied Behavior Analysis, 18,* 17–31.

McGee, G. G., Krantz, P. J., & McClannahan, L. E. (1986). An extension of incidental teaching procedures to reading instruction for autistic children. *Journal of Applied Behavior Analysis, 19,* 147–157.

Miranda-Linne, F., & Melin, L. (1992). Acquisition, generalization, and spontaneous use of color adjectives: A comparison of incidental teaching and traditional discrete-trial procedures for children with autism. *Research in Developmental Disabilities, 13,* 191–210.

Noonan, M. J., & McCormick, L. (1993). *Early intervention in natural environments: Methods and procedures.* Pacific Grove, CA: Brooks/Cole.

Ostrosky, M. M., & Kaiser, A. P. (1991). Preschool classroom environments that promote communication. *Teaching Exceptional Children, 23*(4) 6–10.

Oswald, L. K., Lignugaris/Kraft, B., & West, R. (1990). The effects of incidental teaching on the generalized use of social amenities at school by a mildly handicapped adolescent. *Education and Treatment of Children, 13,* 142–152.

Peterson, P., (2005). *Naturalistic language teaching: Effective procedures for promoting generalization.* Manuscript in preparation.

Peterson, P., Carta, J. J., & Greenwood, C. R. (2005). Teaching enhanced milieu language teaching skills to parents of multiple risk families. *Journal of Early Intervention. 27(2), 94–109.*

Ramey, C. T., & Campbell, F. A. (1992). Poverty, early childhood education, and academic competence: The Abecedarian experiment. In A. Huston (Ed.), *Children in poverty (pp. 190–221).* New York: Cambridge University Press.

Rogers-Warren, A., & Warren, S. F. (1980). Mands for verbalization. *Behavior Modification, 4,* 361–382

Seifert, H., & Schwarz, I. (1991). Treatment effectiveness of large group basic concept instruction with Head Start students. *Language, Speech, and Hearing Services in the Schools, 22,* 60–64.

Spradlin, J. E., & Siegel, G. (1982). Language training in natural and clinical environments. *Journal of Speech and Hearing Disorders, 47,* 2–6.

Stokes, T. F., & Baer, D. M. (1977). An implicit technology of generalization. *Journal of Applied Behavior Analysis, 10,* 349–367.

Sundberg, M. L., & Partington, J. W. (1998). *Teaching language to children with autism or other disabilities.* Pleasant Hill, CA: Behavior Analysts, Inc.

Tannock, R., & Girolametto, L. (1992). Reassessing parent-focused language intervention programs. In S. F. Warren & J. Reichle (Eds.), *Causes and effects in communication and language intervention* (pp. 49–76). Baltimore, MD: Paul H. Brookes.

Warren, S. F. (1988). A behavioral approach to language generalization. *Language, Speech, and Hearing in the Schools, 19,* 292–303.

Warren, S. F. (1992). Facilitating basic vocabulary acquisition with milieu teaching procedures. *Journal of Early Intervention, 16,* 235–251.

Warren, S. F., & Bambara, L. M. (1989). An experimental analysis of milieu language intervention: Teaching the action-object form. *Journal of Speech and Hearing Disorders, 54,* 448–461.

Warren, S. F., & Gazdag, G. (1990). Facilitating early language development with milieu intervention procedures. *Journal of Early Intervention, 14,* 62–86.
Warren, S. F., & Kaiser, A. P. (1986). Incidental language teaching: A critical review. *Journal of Speech and Hearing Disorders, 51,* 291–299.
Warren, S. F., McQuarter, R. J., & Rogers-Warren, A. P. (1984). The effects of mands and models on the speech of unresponsive language-delayed preschool children. *Journal of Speech and Hearing Disorders, 49,* 43–52.
Warren, S. F., Yoder, P. J., Gazdag, G. E., Kim, K., & Jones, H. A. (1993). Facilitating prelinguistic communication skills in young children with developmental delay. *Journal of Speech and Hearing Research, 36,* 83–97.
Wetherby, A. M., & Prizant, B. M. (1992). Profiling young children's communicative competence. In S. F. Warren & J. Reichle (Eds.), *Causes and effects in communication and language intervention* (pp. 217–253). Baltimore, MD: Paul H. Brookes.

Insights on Learning Disabilities 2(2), 59–73, 2005

The Relation Between Self-Esteem and Learning Disabilities in Young Children in a Greek Primary School

Evaggelia T. Adam, M.Ed.
Thessaloniki, Greece;

The purpose of this study was first to explore whether Greek children with LD exhibit low self-esteem; second whether a correlation exists between school competence and the development of self-esteem, or whether other competencies of the child (non-academic) impede his/her self-esteem enhancement. The role of children's age and gender was also examined. Results indicated that Greek children with LD do not exhibit low self-esteem. On the contrast to self-esteem, they revealed a low scholastic competence, however not low enough to affect self-esteem's development. Correlations were found mainly between scholastic competence, peer relationships and self-esteem. Minor gender differences in self-esteem's development appeared favoring girls, while in relation to age, self-esteem appeared to be rather stable.

According to several researchers, a child's self-concept in different areas that are judged to be of great significance to the child, such as academic self-concept, may affect the development of a child's self-esteem (Crozier, Rees, Morris-Beattie, & Bellin, 1999; Harter & Pike, 1984; Kloomok, & Cosden, 1994; Leondari, 1993; Makri-Mpotsari, 2001a). Some researchers view self-concept as a multidimensional phenomenon with multiple and relatively independent aspects (e.g. Harter, 1985; Tesser & Campbell, 1983 [as cited in Kloomok & Cosden]). For example, there is a possibility that a child's general self-esteem may not be the same as the child's academic self-concept or academic self-esteem (Huntington & Bender, 1993).

The self-perceptions of children with LD have been of particular interest to researchers in the last twenty years (Gurney, 1988). A common notion is that children with LD, because of the academic difficulties they face, will have lower self-perceptions than their peers, affecting their sense of competence. This in turn could lead to feelings of low self-worth and self-esteem (Cordell, 1999).

Moreover, children with LD usually live under the threat of being labeled as "lazy," "obstinate" or "stupid" both by their teachers and their peers. Being labeled (Makri-Mpotsari, 2001a) or even worse bullied by their peers (Eaude, 1999; O'Moore, 2000) reduces or damages the self-esteem of students with

LD. There is an argument, however, for suggesting that there will not be a demonstrable difference between those with and without LD, because of the effects of intervening factors, such as special education, inclusive education, social skills training, and self-esteem enhancement. (Gurney, 1988; Humphrey, 2002, 2003; Humphrey & Mullins, 2002).

In reference to specific LD, it is advocated that academic failure can negatively affect self-concept (Goor, McKnab, & Davison-Aviles, 1995). Children with LD are likely to demonstrate low self-esteem when they do not manage to capitalize on their abilities and overcome their weaknesses (Miles & Varma, 1995).

Studies into the self-esteem of children with LD, however, reveal inconsistent findings. Some studies have found that the self-concept and self-esteem of children with LD are more negative (Bear, Clever, & Proctor, 1991; DeFrancesco & Taylor, 1985), while others report no difference between groups (Kistner, Haskett, White, & Robbins, 1987; Winne, Woodlands, & Wong, 1982).

In recent research on the self-esteem of students categorized as LD, Humphrey (2002) tested the self-esteem of children with dyslexia attending mainstream schools, children with LD, and children without LD with the "semantic differential" method adopted by Richmond (1984). Results indicated that dyslexia has an effect on children's self-esteem, as significant main effects were found for self-esteem of reading, writing, and spelling ability, intelligence, English ability, neatness, popularity, and importance. Additionally, as with Thomson's (1990) research, the significant differences were mostly between the dyslexic mainstream group and the control group, and the dyslexic mainstream group and the LD group, especially for writing and reading ability. For the other scales, the differences found were between the dyslexic mainstream group and one (but not both) of the two other groups.

The current study concentrated on the presumption that children do not feel equally competent in every skill domain and was designed to investigate whether poor academic attainment or another domain was responsible for low self-esteem in children with LD.

The study focused on selected intrinsic and extrinsic factors associated with the formation of self-esteem in children with LD, such as gender and age differences, as well as the role of low academic attainment, scholastic competence, and other domains not related to the academic profile of children with LD. Under this hypothesis and concerns around self-esteem and LD, the following research questions were addressed.

- Do children with LD display low self-esteem?
- Are there any gender differences in the development of self-esteem in children with LD?

- Are there any age differences in the development of self-esteem in children with LD?
- Are low academic attainment and low academic self-concept (scholastic competence) factors that lead to the development of low self-esteem in children with LD? Or do other domains of self-concept (Social Acceptance, Athletic Competence, Physical Appearance, Behavioral Conduct) play equally important roles in self-esteem development?

METHOD

Participants

The data were drawn from a sample of 32 students (18 boys, 14 girls) with LD from Grades 4 to 6 in two public elementary schools of northern and southern Thessaloniki, Greece. The students ranged from 9.5 to 12 years of age. The students had been diagnosed as having LD through Athena Test, a multithematic test consisting of 14 scales and being used for the identification of children with LD by the Greek L.E.As.

The selection of the schools and consequently the whole sample was based on the method of convenience sampling. Worth noting, however, is that the criteria set for this specific research were met, and the schools chosen assured that the sample consisted of children from a variety of social and economic backgrounds. Nonetheless, the method of random sampling would possibly be more appropriate.

Measures-Instruments

The Greek version of Self-Perception Profile for Children

Harter's (1985) (as cited in Kloomek & Cosden, 1994) Self Perception Profile for Children (SPPC), in its Greek version (PATEM II), standardized in the Greek student population by Makri-Mpotsari (2001b), was used to assess the self-esteem of children with learning disabilities. This instrument was chosen as it is widely used (Crozier et al., 1999; Makri-Mpotsari, 2001a, 2001b; Muldoon, 2000; Rossman & Rosenberg, 1993) with good cross-cultural reliability and validity (Harter; Muldoon, 2000). Moreover, it was chosen among others as it was already translated, properly adjusted and standardized to the needs of the Greek population, and successfully used by Makri-Mpotsari, 2001a, with good reliability and validity.

PATEM II (Makri-Mpotsari, 2001b) has 30 items consisting of 5 items per scale, for each of the six scales. Children respond using a structured alternative format for each question, a format designed to overcome the response bias evident in forced-choice paradigms, and to minimize the socially desired answers. As such, children are presented with two conflicting statements and are asked first to decide which of the two statements applies best to them. For example:

Some children feel they are very good at their school work.	BUT	Other children worry about whether they can do the school work assigned to them.

When children have decided which statement they agree with, they are then asked to indicate, by ticking one of two boxes alongside the statement they have chosen, whether the statement is "really true" or "sort of true" for them.

Procedure

Consent was obtained prior to the participation of children with LD by all interested parties (schools' headmasters, parents, teachers, and children), and ample explanations for the research's purposes, as well its procedures, were given. Furthermore, the research was conducted approximately six months after the beginning of the school year, so the children already felt familiar with their school environment.

Children completed the Greek version of the SPPC (PATEM II) instrument in their classes. The classes ranged in size from 15 to 30 pupils. To avoid discrimination and stigmatization of the children participating in the study, all the children in the classroom completed the questionnaires. All items were read aloud to the children and it was made clear to them that they should tick only one of the given squares to each question, and seek the researcher's help when needed.

Data Analysis

To reach data analysis of the Greek version of the Harter's Self Perception Profile for Children, the writer used the PATEM II manual (Makri-Mpotsari, 2001b) to obtain self-esteem and self-concept scores of children with LD. Based on that, if the self-esteem or self-concept mean/average scores of the child are below 2.5, then the child is considered to display low self-esteem or low self-concept respectively. The higher the child's mean/average self-esteem and self-concept scores are, the higher the child's self-esteem and self-concept are considered to be. Additionally, descriptive statistics (Makri-Mpotsari, 2001b; Oppenheim, 1992; Robson, 2002) were also used to answer the study's research questions. Furthermore, the Pearson test (Oppenheim, 1992; Robson, 2002) was used to examine the correlation between the different areas of dyslexic children's self-concept and their self-esteem, in order to find out whether a specific area of self-concept (scholastic concept, or other areas of self-concept) affects the development of self-esteem.

RESULTS

- Do children with LD display low self-esteem?

  Table 1 indicates that children with LD do not exhibit a low self-esteem. On the contrary, it could be well supported that they present a negative scholastic self-concept, when compared with the other areas of self-concept. Worth noting is the fact that physical appearance presents the same mean score with self-esteem (m = 2.8). In general, self-esteem and all the areas of the self-concept scale, apart from the scholastic competence, appear above 2.5, and no great differences between self-esteem and self-concept scales are observed.

Table 1

Means/averages of Self-Concept and Self-Esteem of Children with LD

Scale	Mean/average
Scholastic competence	2.4
Peer relationships/acceptance	2.9
Athletic competence	3.0
Physical appearance	2.8
Behavior/conduct	3.1
SELF-ESTEEM	2.8

- Are there any gender differences in the development of self-esteem in children with LD?

  Data analysis, in general, revealed that the majority of children with LD do not appear to exhibit low self-esteem; however a third of the sample (31.25%) did demonstrate low self-esteem. Compared to boys, more girls (35.71%) appeared to demonstrate low self-esteem, while the lowest self-esteem score was displayed in the boys' group. No significant differences (r = 0.07) were found, however, between the two genders in regard to their self-esteem formation. Nonetheless, according to the scoring guide, none of the mean averages of the two genders' identify a low self-esteem. In general, only in the behavior/conduct scale the difference reaches the 0.5 units, with girls displaying a higher level of behavior/conduct competence than boys. Boys, appear to have better results than girls in the physical appearance and scholastic competence scales.

- Are there any age differences in the development of self-esteem in children with LD?

  Comparing the age of the children to the manifestation of low self-esteem, it can be deduced that the fourth-graders appear to be the ones that most lack self-confidence (15.62%). The lowest self-esteem score, however, is revealed in fifth-graders. Otherwise, self-esteem appears to be rather stable between the age span, ranging form 2.84 (5th grade) to 2.87 (4th grade), and 2.88 (6th grade). In the areas of self-concept, however, differences are manifested, with the greater difference presented in peer relationships (0.36 points) and the behavior/conduct (0.38 points) between the fourth-graders and the fifth-graders, favoring the latter. Additionally, great differences are also seen between the fifth-graders and the sixth-graders in the areas of scholastic competence (0.35 points) and behavior/conduct (0.60 points), favoring fifth-graders, while in athletic competence (0.36 points), favoring sixth-graders. Furthermore, between the fourth-graders and the sixth-graders the greater difference is presented in scholastic competence (0.39 points) and in peer relationships (0.32 points), favoring the fourth- graders. Worth noting is the fact that in scholastic competence a decrease is revealed as the age increases.

- Are low academic attainment and low academic self-concept (scholastic competence) factors that lead to the development of low self-esteem in children with LD? Or do other domains of self-concept (Social Acceptance, Athletic Competence, Physical Appearance, Behavioral Conduct) play equally important roles in self-esteem development?

Table 2

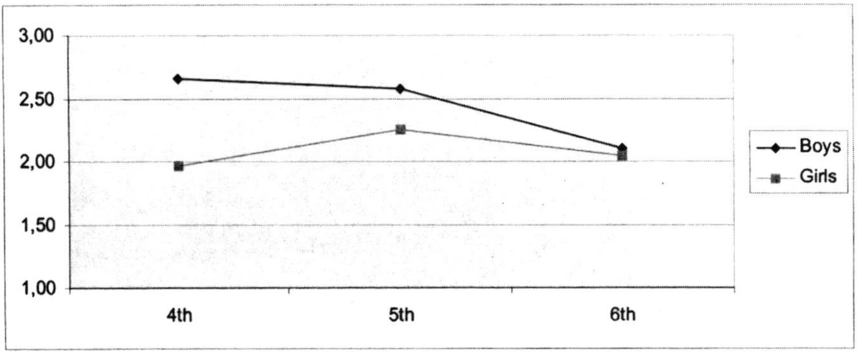

Figure 1. Means of scholastic competence per sex and grade

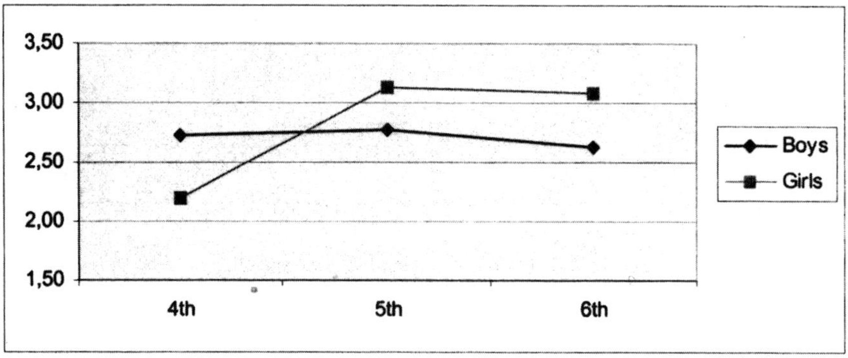

Figure 2. Means of peer relationships/acceptance per sex and grade

The Correlation of Self-esteem (Pearson r) With the Different Areas of Self-concept of Children With LD.

Areas of Self-concept	Pearson *r*
Scholastic competence	0.44
Peer relationships/acceptance	0.41
Athletic competence	0.23
Physical appearance	0.12
Behavior/conduct	0.36

Examining carefully the data of Table 2 it can be asserted that the self-esteem of children with LD is positively correlated with all the areas of self-concept examined by the questionnaire. The area that seems to affect the children's self-esteem development the most is their perception about their scholastic competence (r = 0.44). Peer relationships (r = 0.41) and behavior/conduct (r = 0.36) also appear to play a significant role in the development of self-esteem, while physical appearance (r = 0.12) and athletic competence (r = 0.23) are demonstrated not to affect significantly self-esteem's course of development.

Additionally, regarding the gender and the correlation of self-esteem to the different areas of self-concept, it can be deduced that for girls scholastic competence (r = 0.60) positively affects the development of self-esteem, whereas for boys, peer relationships (r = 0.66) are more influential in the development of self-esteem. Surprisingly, athletic competence seems not to affect significantly the development of self-esteem in either gender.

Table 3

The correlation of Self-esteem to the Different Areas of Self-concept, by Gender for Both Schools

Areas of Self-concept	Pearson *r*	
	Gender	
	Boys	Girls
Scholastic competence	0.32	0.60
Peer relationships/acceptance	0.66	0.21
Athletic competence	0.01	0.40
Physical appearance	0.16	0.07
Behavior/conduct	0.43	0.35

Respectively, in accordance to the correlation of self-esteem to the different areas of self-concept that can be noticed through different ages, it can be inferred that peer relationships (r = 0.76) and behavior/conduct (r = 0.68) are more positively correlated to self-esteem's development than the other areas of self-concept, for the fourth-graders. The same areas of self-concept appear to be more positively correlated to self-esteem, for the sixth-graders as well (peer relationships, r = 0.55, behavior/conduct, r = 0.60). On the contrary, the fifth-graders seem to be more affected by their scholastic competence for the formation of their positive self-esteem. Data for the fifth-graders also demonstrate negative correlations between self-esteem and peer relationships (r = –0.09), as well as behavior/conduct (r = –0.10). Additionally, negative correlations between self-esteem and areas of self-concept are also presented in sixth-graders, in athletic competence (r = –0.12) and physical appearance (r = –0.09).

Table 4

The Correlation of Self-esteem to Areas of Self-concept, by Grade for Both Schools

Areas of Self-concept	Grade		
	4th	5th	6th
Scholastic competence	0.35	0.71	0.31
Peer relationships/acceptance	0.76	-0.09	0.55
Athletic competence	0.49	0.47	-0.12
Physical appearance	0.09	0.31	-0.09
Behavior/conduct	0.68	-0.10	0.60

Discussion and Conclusions

The aim of this study was to investigate whether Greek children with LD present low self-esteem. Moreover, the study attempted to reveal the factors that contribute to the construction and development of the self-esteem of children with LD and, furthermore to highlight the possible gender and age/grade differences that may affect self-esteem's development.

Findings of the current studies highlighted that the majority of the children with LD (69.75%) were found to demonstrate self-esteem above the average (2.5), while one third of the children were found to exhibit lower rates of self-esteem. This finding can be interpreted adopting Harter's (1983) view on the multidimensionality of the self, that recognizes that an individual's level of self-esteem can vary from one domain to another, so that someone with low academic self-esteem/concept might have a more positive self-esteem where performance in sports is concerned. In line with that interpretation and the study's findings, Kloomok and Cosden (1994) reported that the majority of children with specific reading disabilities demonstrated a negative self-concept (85%) while on the contrary, they presented a positive global self-esteem (67%), indicating that children with specific learning disability (SLD) tend to feel good about themselves in general, but feel less adequate about their scholastic competence. Additionally, previous research (Priel & Leshem, 1990; Renick & Harter, 1989), also reached the conclusion that children with SLD did not appear to have low self-esteem, but a low scholastic competence instead.

In reference to the self-concept of children with LD, the findings suggest that all the areas of self-concept, but one, were above 2.5. This fact implies that children with LD in general view themselves positively, under all the mentioned areas of their lives. Nonetheless, in spite of the fact that children with LD appear to have a rather high self-esteem (m = 2.8), as well as athletic competence (3.0) and behavior/ conduct (3.1), they seem to lack confidence and view themselves negatively in terms of scholastic competence. Such a finding is consistent with several researchers that reach the same conclusions (Boetsch, Green, & Pennington, 1996; Casey, Levy, Brown, & Brooks-Gunn, 1992; Kloomok & Cosden, 1994; Riddick, 1996; Riddick, Farmer, & Sterling, 1997).

In regard to gender, it can be deduced that girls (35.71%) appear to have lower self-esteem than boys (27.77%) by 7.94%. However, according to the means of self-esteem development between the two genders there does not appear to exist a significant difference, as the difference is 0.07 points. This finding is consistent with additional research findings that reveal that there are not remarkable differences in self-esteem's development between the two genders (Carlock, 1999; Elbaum & Vaughn, 2001). Nonetheless, in regard to the low self-esteem group of children, the difference of 7.94% between the boys and girls, regardless of the fact that it is not significant, it can be assumed that the minor difference observed may be due to the slightly different perceptions that girls have of themselves when constructing their self-esteem. The writer's estimation is congruent with the Dusek and Flaherty (1981) review which reported differences in specific areas of self-concept that were consistent with gender stereotypes: Boys had higher self-concepts in masculinity and achievement/leadership, and lower self-concepts in congeniality/sociability. Similarly, Marsh, Barnes, Cairns, and Tidman (1984) found gender differences favoring boys in self-concept of physical ability and favoring girls in reading. In line with the above mentioned studies, this study revealed that boys perceived themselves as more competent mainly in the areas of academic competence and physical appearance, while girls were found to claim being more competent mainly in peer relationships/acceptance.

In terms of age/grade level, data showed no obvious pattern of differences in the development of the self-esteem of children with LD. However, fourth-graders (15.62%) appeared to demonstrate a lower self-esteem compared to the fifth-(6.25%), and the sixth-graders (9.37%). Worth noticing is the fact that children with LD seem to improve their self-esteem as they grow older. This fact could possibly be attributed to the positive effects special education has on them. The fact that age/grade appears not to affect self-esteem's development can be interpreted by research that reveals that an individual's evaluations of him/herself over the course of time are rather stable (Swann, 1996). Battle

(1990) claimed that once an individual's level of self-esteem is well established, it becomes rather difficult to alter and therefore remains relatively stable over time. Therefore, with increasing age, young people's perceptions of themselves become increasingly stable (Alsaker & Olweus, 1992).This may be due to individuals' inclination for self-verification, an inclination that is attributed to their desire for precaution and control (Baumeister, 1993; Epstein, 1991 [as cited in Makri-Mpotsari, 2001a]).

Concerning how the different areas of self-concept develop in children with LD in relation to their age/grade, it can be deduced that as children with LD grow older their perceptions of their scholastic competence and behavior/conduct seem to fall. On the contrary, their perceptions of peer relationships/acceptance and physical appearance appear to rise. Such findings could possibly mean that as children grow older they view themselves more realistically (Makri-Mpotsari, 2001a), as they are also affected by the significant others' opinions about them (i.e. their academic ability and their behavior). Additionally, as they grow older, children develop an ability to process information about the self in a more abstract and differential manner (Case, 1996; Harter, 1990 [as cited in Muldoon 2000]), and therefore pay more attention to their sociability and physical appearance, areas that help them view themselves positively, and become more sociable and likable to others (significant others). Perhaps, children with LD consider peer relationships and physical appearance to play a more significant role in the way that significant others (especially when these significant others are their peers) view them.

Another major theme of this study was the correlation between self-esteem and academic competence, or other areas of self-concept. The aim was mainly to find out whether children with LD perceive their academic failure and furthermore whether their negative perceptions of their academic attainment/competence lead to the development of a low self-esteem. According to the study's findings scholastic competence appeared to be positively correlated with self-esteem, a fact that seemed to be consistent with previous research in the same area (Chapman & Tunmer, 2002 [as cited in Meltzer, Katzir, Miller, Reddy, & Roditi, 2004]; Humphrey, 2002; Riddick et al., 1997). Additionally, from the data analysis, as well as literature review (Humphrey, 2002; Kloomok & Cosden, 1994; Riddick, 1996), it was revealed that another factor that seems to affect self-esteem's development is peer relationships. This finding could be interpreted based on Meads' (1902) and Cooley's (1934) theory of significant others, and the effect they have in our lives. Juvonen and Wentzel, (1996) and Renick and Harter (1989) also reveal a positive relationship between physical appearance and self-esteem development of children with LD. Nonetheless, such a relationship was not confirmed by this study.

Considering the role of gender in self-esteem correlation to the different areas of self-concept, it can be deduced that girls appeared to be more affected by their perceptions about their scholastic competence in their self-esteem establishment (r = 0.60), whereas boys were affected, as indicated, by their peer relationships (r = 0.66). This difference between the two genders has to do with the social stereotypes that expect girls to achieve at school and boys to be more sociable (Makri-Mpotsari, 2001a).

In line with the age/grade and self-esteem's correlation to the different areas of self-concept, fourth-graders' self-esteem seems to be mainly predicted by three domains of self-competence: peer relationships (r = 0.76), behavior/conduct (r = 0.68), and athletic competence (r = 0.49). Additionally, fifth-graders' self-esteem is mainly affected by their scholastic competence (r = 0.71) and athletic competence (r = 0.47), while sixth-graders' self-esteem is shown to be positively correlated with peer relationships (r = 0.55) and behavior/conduct (r = 0.60). As well, negative correlations, of no great importance, were found between self-esteem and behavior/conduct (r = -0.10) and peer relationships (r = -0.09) in fifth grade, and athletic competence (r = -0.12), and physical appearance (r = -0.09) in sixth grade. The negative correlation between peer relationships and self-esteem could possibly be interpreted on the basis that as peer relationships develop, the children start making comparisons between themselves and their peers discovering that they are in a disadvantaged condition, which ultimately leads to unfavorable opinions of themselves. The negative correlation between the child's behavior and his/her self-esteem can be explained in the same context. By demonstrating poor behavior, the child tends to feel secure, as he/she attributes all his/her disadvantages, misfortunes, and failures to that behavior. Through that unorthodox way children seem to protect their self-esteem, something that is in accord with their age (fourth grade) as they still have not started to view themselves realistically and their views are governed by exaggerations (Makri-Mpotsari, 2001a). Similarly, the negative correlation between athletic competence, physical appearance and self-esteem may be attributed to the fact that children perceive themselves to be more competent in athletics and in appearance than in areas that are highly approved of by their parents, teachers, and eventually their peers, and their whole social surrounding as they grow older. That may be the reason why those correlations make their appearance in the sixth grade when the child starts to realize the importance of being academically competent.

Scholastic competence appeared to be positively correlated to self-esteem, while peer relationships seemed to affect the development of self-esteem as well. This finding is inconsistent with the high levels of self-esteem that Greek children with LD presented. Nonetheless, peer relationships also were shown to be interconnected with self-esteem's establishment. This could possibly mean either that peer relationships affect their self-esteem more, or that despite the fact that they acknowledge their inefficiency in the area of academics, they deliberately underestimate its importance to protect their self-esteem (Makri-Mpotsari, 2001a).

Gender differences in low self-esteem appeared only by 7.94%, favoring girls, which could possibly be accounted for by the different concepts/perceptions that boys and girls use as a source of reference when constructing their self-esteem, in line with the socially acceptable gender stereotypes. In general, however, there were no reported significant differences between males' and females' self-esteem development. In summary, although there appears to be little evidence of gender differences in total self-concept and self-esteem of children with LD, there do appear to be systematic gender differences in particular dimensions of self-concept that are consistent with gender stereotypes (Dusek & Flaherty, 1981).

For most students a decrease in self-esteem occurred by the fifth grade (age 10 to 11), while a decrease in the academic self-concept occurred by sixth grade (age 11 to 12). This decrease, however, was not of significant importance. In general, it can be asserted that the academic self-concept followed an ongoing decline with increasing age among students with LD, which can be interpreted on the basis that their actual self-awareness and metacognition rise with age (Makri-Mpotasi, 2001a; Meltzer, Reddy et al., 2004). On the contrary, with reference to self-esteem there was a small increase in sixth grade. On the whole, the self esteem of children with LD appeared to be rather stable, and any small increase could possibly be attributed to the positive effects of special education and self-esteem enhancement. The reports of teachers of children with LD in Greece reveal that they believe in the positive contribution that special educational services (i.e. the IEP), as well as self-esteem methods and techniques (i.e. circle time), have in boosting the self-esteem of children with LD.

Overall, this study does advance knowledge about the development of the self-perceptions of Greek children with LD about their self-esteem and the different areas of their self-competence. The current findings suggest that children with LD generally see themselves in a positive light. The findings do not suggest that the majority of students with LD are dysfunctional, have low self-esteem or self-concept. This could be interpreted on the basis that the students of the sample seem to compensate for poor academic concept/performances in nonacademic and extracurricular activities, enabling their self-esteem to remain reasonably intact, and thereby explain the "normal" self-esteem rate reported by the Greek students with LD.

Limitations of the study

While this study has avoided many of the potential pitfalls associated with research in this area, a number of issues merit consideration. This research, though enhanced by a longitudinal design, would have been strengthened by a larger sample of children. Secondly, it also would be better to include a control group of children so as to better examine the relationship between self-esteem and academic achievement. Additionally, the link between actual academic performance and self-concept and self-esteem is unclear as the questionnaire used for self-esteem and self-concept assessment did not include questions specific to different areas of academic ability (i.e. math, writing, reading, spelling, etc.).

Future research should attempt to directly establish the relationship between academic attainment and self-esteem and self-concept, to further understanding of the complex relationship between children's evaluation of the role of their academic competence to the development of their self-esteem. Future research would also benefit from a larger sample, accessed from a greater number of schools. This would make the research findings more reliable as the writer would be able to claim that the findings are indicative of and generalized to the population. Additionally, further research could find out and compare the different school-based interventions existing for the enhancement of self-esteem and self-concept of students with LD. As educators, if we claim that we really want to help children with LD to be healthily adjusted in society, finding and introducing new ways of self-esteem enhancement should be our main interest.

References

Alsaker, F. D., & Olweus, D. (1992). Stability of global self-evaluations in early adolescence: A cohort longitudinal study. *Journal of Research on Adolescence, 2,* 123–145.

Battle, J. (1990). *Self-esteem: The new revolution.* Canada: James Battles.

Baumeister, R. F. (1993). Understanding the inner nature of low self-esteem: Uncertainty, fragile, protective, and conflicted. In R. F. Baumeister (Ed.), *Self-esteem: The puzzle of low self-regard* (pp. 201–218). New York: Plenum.

Bear. G. C., Clever, A., & Proctor, W. A. (1991). Self-perceptions of nonhandicapped children and children with learning disabilities in integrated classes. *The Journal of Special Education, 24,* 409–426.

Boetsch, E. A., Green, P. A., & Pennington, B. F. (1996). Psychological correlates of dyslexia across the life span. *Development and Psychopathology, 8,* 539–562.

Carlock, C. J. (1999). Enhancing self-esteem: A model for change. In C. J. Carlock (Ed.), *Enhancing self-esteem.* London: Taylor and Francis.

Case, R. (1996). Classic and contemporary models of children's cognitive structures: A brief overview. *Monographs of the Society for Research in Child Development, 61*(1–2), 189–214.

Casey, R., Levy, S., Brown, K., & Brooks-Gunn, J. (1992). Impaired emotional health in children with mild reading disability. *Developmental and Behavioral Pediatrics, 13*(4), 256–260.

Cooley, C. (1902). *Human nature and the social order.* New York: Charles Schribner.

Cordell, A. S. (1999). Self-esteem in children, in C. J. Carlock (Ed.), *Enhancing self-esteem.* London: Taylor and Francis.
Crozier, R. W., Rees, V., Morris-Beattie, A., & Bellin, W. (1999). Streaming, self-esteem and friendship within a Comprehensive School. *Educational Psychology in Practice, 15*(2), 128–134.
DeFrancesco, J .J., & Taylor, J. (1985). Dimensions of self-concept in primary and middle school learning disabled and nondisabled students. *Child Study Journal, 15,* 99–105.
Dusek, J. B., & Flaherty, J. F. (1981). The development of self-concept during adolescent years. *Monographs of the Society for Research in Child Development, 46,* (4, Serial No. 191).
Eaude, T. (1999). *Learning difficulties: Dyslexia, bullying and other issues,* London: Letts Educational.
Elbaum, B. & Vaughn, S. (2001). School-based interventions to enhance the self-concept of students with learning disabilities: A meta-analysis. *The Elementary School Journal, 101*(3), 303–329.
Epstein, S. (1991). Cognitive-experiential self theory: Implications for developmental psychology. In Makri-Mpotsari, E. (2001a). *Self-concept and self-esteem: Models, development, functional role and assessment.* Athens: Ellinika Grammata.
Goor, M. B., Mcknab, P. A., & Davison-Aviles, R. (1995). Counseling individuals with learning disabilities. *Advances in Special Education, 9,* 99–118.
Gurney, P. (1988). *Self-esteem in children with special educational needs.* London: Routledge.
Harter, S. (1983). Developmental perspectives on the self-system. In E. M. Hetherington (Ed.), *Handbook of child psychology: Socialization, personality and social development* (4th ed., Vol. 4, pp. 275–386). New York: Wiley.
Harter, S., & Pike, R. (1984). The pictorial scale of perceived competence and social acceptance for young children. *Child Development, 55*(6), 1969–1982.
Humphrey, N. (2002). Teacher and pupil ratings of self-esteem in developmental dyslexia. *British Journal of Special Education, 29*(1), 29–36.
Humphrey, N. (2003). Dyslexia: Facilitating a positive sense of self in pupils with dyslexia: The role of teachers and peers. *Supporting Learning, 18*(3), 130–136.
Humphrey, N., & Mullins, M. P. (2002). Personal constructs and attribution for academic success and failure in dyslexia. *British Journal of Special Education, 29*(4), 196–203.
Huntington, D. D., & Bender, W. N. (1993). Adolescents with learning disabilities at risk? Emotional well-being, depression, suicide. *Journal of Learning Disabilities, 26*(3), 159–166.
Juvonen, J., & Wentzel, K. R. (Eds.). (1996). *Social motivation: Understanding children's school adjustment.* New York: Cambridge University Press.
Kistner, J., Haskett, M., White, K., & Robbins, F. (1987). Perceived competence and self-worth of learning disabled and normally achieving students. *Learning Disability Quarterly, 10,* 37–44.
Kloomok, S., & Cosden, M. (1994). Self-Concept in children with learning disabilities: The relationship between global self-concept, academic "discounting", nonacademic self-concept, and perceived social support. *Learning Disability Quarterly, 17,* 140–153.
Leondari, A. (1993). Comparability of self-concept among normal achievers, low achievers and children with learning difficulties. *Educational Studies, 19*(3), 357–371.
Makri-Mpotsari, E. (2001a). *Self-concept and self-esteem: Models, development, functional role and assessment.* Athens: Ellinika Grammata.

Makri-Mpotsari, E. (2001b). Manual: The Way I Perceive Myself II (PATEM II). A questionnaire about the self-concept's and self-esteem's assessment of 4th-,5th-, and 6th-elementary graders. *A manual of the Greek version of Self-Perception Profile For Children (Harter).* Athens: Ellinika Gramatta.

Marsh, H. W., Barnes, J, Cairns, L., & Tidman, M. (1984). The Self Description Questionnaire (SDQ): Age effects in the structure and level of self-concept for preadolescent children. *Journal of Educational Psychology, 76,* 940–956.

Mead, G. H. (1934) *Mind, self and society.* University of Chicago Press.

Meltzer, L., Katzir, T., Miller, L., Reddy, R., & Roditi, B. (2004). Academic self-perceptions, effort, and strategy use in students with learning disabilities: Changes over time. *Learning Disabilities Research & Practice, 19*(2), 99–108.

Meltzer, L., Reddy, R., Sales Polica, L., Roditi, B., Sayer, J., & Theokas, Ch. (2004). Positive and negative self-perceptions: Is there a cyclical relationship between teachers' and students' perceptions of effort, strategy use, and academic performance? *Learning Disabilities Research & Practice, 19*(1), 33–34.

Miles, T., & Varma, V. (1995). An overview. In T. R. Miles & V. Varma (Eds.), *Dyslexia and stress* (pp. 112–123). London: Whurr.

Muldoon, T. O. (2000). Social group membership and self-perceptions in Northern Irish children: A longitudinal study. *British Journal of Developmental Psychology, 18,* 65–80.

O'Moore, M. (2000). Critical issues for teacher training to counter bullying and victimization in Ireland. *Aggressive Behaviour, 26*(1), 99–111.

Oppenheim, A. N. (1992). *Questionnaire design, interviewing and attitude measurement.* London: Pinter.

Priel, B., & Leshem, T. (1990). Self-perceptions of first- and second-grade children with learning disabilities. *Journal of Learning Disabilities, 23,* 637–642.

Renick, M. J., & Harter, S. (1989). Impact of social comparisons on the developing self-perceptions of learning disabled students. *Journal of Educational Psychology, 81,* 631–638.

Richmond, M. J. (1984). The self concept of academically able and less able children in a comprehensive school-a comparative study. *Remedial Education, 19*(2), 57–58.

Riddick, B. (1996). *Living with dyslexia.* London: Routledge.

Riddick, B., Farmer, M., & Sterling, C. (1997). *Students and dyslexia: Growing up with a specific learning difficulty.* London: Whurr.

Robson, C. (2002). *Real world research: A resource for social scientists and practitioner-researchers* (2nd ed.). Oxford: Blackwell.

Rossman, B .B .R., & Rosenberg, M. S. (1993). Family stress and functioning in children: The moderating effects of children's beliefs about their control over parental conflict. *Journal of Child Psychology and Psychiatry, 33*(4), 699–715.

Swann, W. B., Jr. (1996). *Self-traps.* New York: Freeman.

Thomson, M. E. (1990). *Develpomental dyslexia.* London: Whurr.

Winne, P. H., Woodlands, M. J., & Wong, B.Y. L. (1982). Comparability of self-concept among learning disabled, normal, and gifted students. *Journal of Learning Disabilities, 15,* 470–475.

Author's Notes

Correspondence concerning this article should be addressed to: Evaggelia T. Adam, 7 M. Alexandrou, 546 40 Thessaloniki, Greece; e-mail: adamsped@yahoo.gr.